Changemakers

Changemakers

The Industrious Future of the Digital Economy

Adam Arvidsson

polity

The right of Adam Arvidsson to be identified as Author of this Work has been asserted in accordance with the UK Copyright, Designs and Patents Act 1988.

First published in 2019 by Polity Press

Polity Press
65 Bridge Street
Cambridge CB2 1UR, UK

Polity Press
101 Station Landing
Suite 300
Medford, MA 02155, USA

ISBN-13: 978-1-5095-3889-8
ISBN-13: 978-1-5095-3890-4 (pb)

A catalogue record for this book is available from the British Library.

Typeset in 10.5 on 12 pt Sabon
by Fakenham Prepress Solutions, Fakenham, Norfolk NR21 8NL
Printed and bound in Great Britain by CPI Group (UK) Ltd, Croydon

The publisher has used its best endeavours to ensure that the URLs for external websites referred to in this book are correct and active at the time of going to press. However, the publisher has no responsibility for the websites and can make no guarantee that a site will remain live or that the content is or will remain appropriate.

Every effort has been made to trace all copyright holders, but if any have been overlooked the publisher will be pleased to include any necessary credits in any subsequent reprint or edition.

For further information on Polity, visit our website:
politybooks.com

Contents

Acknowledgements

This book is the outcome of more than a decade of research on creative industries, freelance professionals, commons-based peer production, start-ups, social enterprises and other aspects of the digital economy. Most of the research was done during my tenure at the University of Milan. I thank all the people who have taken part in that vibrant research community over the years, and in particular Massimo Airoldi, Carolina Bandinelli, Stefania Barina, Davide Beraldo, Tiziano Bonini, Alessandro Caliandro, Elanor Colleoni, Alberto Cossu, Maitrayee Deka, Alessandro Delfanti, Alessandro Gandini, Alessandro Gerosa, Vincenzo Luisse, Bertram Niessen, Zoe Romano and Chiara Russo. Special thanks go to Luisa Leonini, Alex Giordano, Michel Bauwens, Andrea Fumagalli and Giampaolo Capisani who provided a constant source of inspiration and enthusiasm. I thank Jack Qiu for hosting me at the Chinese University of Hong Kong, and Eva Illouz for inviting me to give a graduate seminar at the Ecole des hautes études en sciences sociales, where I was able to put together a first outline of the argument. I finished the manuscript during my first year of tenure at the University of Naples Federico II and I thank all my colleagues there for providing a truly stimulating scholarly environment.

1

To Change the World:
On Industrious Modernity

Our times are marked by a *pessimism of the intellect and an optimism of the will*, to use an old quote that Leftists sometimes throw around. Our intellectual pessimism manifests itself in the fact that no one seems to have a serious alternative to our present predicament. Our wilful optimism means that, despite the absence of alternatives, there is a general desire for change.

To *Change the World* has become the motto of a new generation. University-educated knowledge workers are toiling away in start-ups and social enterprises, working in peer-production projects and on new crypto ventures that they hope will have an impact beyond the, often elusive, prospect of economic gain. Even when they work in corporate careers, the hope is that their efforts will contribute to some overall transformation. From the downright fraudulent (as when the desire for change is appropriated in slogans of corporate organizations whose aims are far from progressive), via the sometimes silly (like Post-it workshops) to the sincere and earnest toil of many, to be a *Changemaker* has become a common aspiration.[1]

Clearly, the world needs changing. Virtually all serious observers agree that if we go on like this, the future will be grim. But what to change the world into? As of yet, nobody has envisioned a viable alternative to a social model in what appears to be terminal decline, much less any realistic strategy for confronting an ecological crisis of potentially game-changing dimensions.

Industrial modernity – the experience of modernity that prevailed until around the mid-1970s – also valued change. Indeed, change has been at the core of the modern experience ever since it came around. In his classic work, with the appropriate title, borrowed from Marx and Engel's *The Communist Manifesto*, *All that is Solid Melts into Air*, Marshall Berman, the perhaps most famous theorist of modernity, described this condition as one of constant flux: 'To be modern is to find ourselves in an environment that promises us adventure, power, joy, growth, transformation of ourselves and the world – and, at the same time, that threatens to destroy everything we have, everything we know, everything we are.' The difference is that in industrial modernity, change came with a blueprint; there was a plan for the future, and everyone knew more or less what they were striving for (communism, liberal democracy, national sovereignty, etc.). Today this sense of direction has been lost: we are left with change itself, as something of an empty signifier. We have no idea what this change will lead to or what the resulting future might look like. Yet, for a wide range of people – much wider than the strata of middle-class knowledge workers for whom the label 'Changemakers' was originally designed – there is no doubt that change is necessary.[2]

In part the difficulty in imagining a direction for change results from a virtually complete colonization of the imaginary on the part of commercial culture, and the concomitant decline of politics and what used to be called the 'Public Sphere', a condition that Mark Fisher has called 'capitalist realism' and which I explore further in the next chapter.[3] In part, it results from the radical nature of the ecological crisis ahead: a true singularity in the proper sense of the term, something for which all bets are off, and that we cannot see beyond. But perhaps another reason why we cannot imagine a different future is because it is still early days.

Indeed, to want to change the world without knowing exactly into what is not a historically new condition. It is a feature of what I call *industrious* modernity, a kind of modern experience that has been with us in the past. It accompanied the transition *to* industrial capitalism in the West (and possibly marked other parts of the pre-industrial world as well). Industrious modernity was the experience of the European long sixteenth century (and, to some extent, of the medieval commercial revolution that preceded it). It was the experience of an emerging urban civil society organized around guilds and fraternities and built around new ideas of justice and freedom – of the 'many-headed hydra' of soldiers, sailors, beggars, convicts and other outcasts from a crumbling feudal order who, along with the new commoners, challenged ingrained notions of hierarchy and privilege. Starting with the sixteenth-century German peasant wars, the Protestants united these diverse experiences into a common movement for 'change' that came to dominate the emerging political scene in Northern Europe and the colonial United States. According to Max Weber, the Protestants ushered in industrial modernity though their sheer industriousness, their hard work and self-sacrifice. They strove to improve themselves and the world around them, without really knowing what they wanted to achieve. Instead, their striving was clouded in the mystical concept of a 'divine calling'. Like us, they had only a very vague idea of where they were headed, and they might not have liked the results of their strivings, had they come to know them. They were simply not able to see the future that they were in the process of making. Now a similar experience of industrious modernity is affirming itself again, as the 'iron cage' of industrial modernity is falling apart.[4]

To some extent, the return of industrious modernity is a cultural fact. It is the result of the successive dismantling of the Grand Narratives that marked industrial modernity, like communism, liberal democracy or the affluent consumer society, along with the social movements that they inspired. When there are no great schemes left to give direction, the only way to give political or at least civic significance to one's life is to try to change one's own circumstance, or at the most to do good and to have an impact in some abstract and generic sense. But industrious modernity is also supported by a particular material condition. Life in industrial modernity might have been alienating and boring, a life for *specialists without minds, pleasure-seekers without heart*, as Weber wrote in the concluding pages on his essay on *The Protestant*

Ethic. But at least people's existential security was in some sense shielded. You could toil on in your corporate job faithful that, somehow, in the grand scheme of things, what you did made a difference and contributed to a greater cause. When these grand narratives have evaporated, the 'bullshit' nature of many corporate jobs reveals itself. Indeed, David Graeber, who coined the term, suggests that about 40 per cent of workers in middle management jobs like PR, human resources, brand managers or financial consultants 'feel their jobs are pointless'. Many people now escape such careers if they can, sensing that a bullshit job will not allow them to make the kind of change they desire, or even realize their own ambitions. In addition, a growing number of people are cast out from corporate careers, because of redundancies, because what they do has been outsourced and they are forced to go freelance, or because they were never able to get on the first rung of the ladder in the first place, despite an expensive university degree. To these outcasts the existential threats of a precarious existence have to be faced head on. Industrious modernity is the experience of people who face insecurity without the shield of a corporate organization and ever less of a protective welfare state – people who have to eke out an existence in the middle, between the destitute reality of employment and the safety of a stable career. To 'Change the World' is the politics – or the political unconscious perhaps – of such precarity. It is a way of convincing yourself, rightly or wrongly, that you are doing something valuable and that your life has meaning. The protestant sects that Weber wrote about worked much in the same way.[5]

And this industrious condition is becoming ever more *common*. Indeed, something similar has always been part of the modern experience for ordinary people. Even in the organized societies of industrial modernity, many operated outside of regulated labour markets or secure careers. Think of the family restaurants and small boarding houses that proliferated in European working-class neighbourhoods until quite recently; food carts on the streets of Singapore or Mumbai; the *magliari* from Naples who travelled quite undisturbed between Paris and Berlin peddling knock-off textiles in the middle of World War II; and of course the informal economy offering sometimes illicit goods and services. In the conclusion to his magnum opus on the history of capitalism in the West, Fernand Braudel marvelled at the fact that despite almost half a millennium of increasingly sophisticated capitalist institutions, there remained 'a sort of lower layer of the economy', a competitive economy different from what he considered 'true capitalism'. This industrious economy – small-scale, flexible and semi-formal – has remained more prevalent in some places, like India or Southern Italy, but it was never entirely eradicated even in the highly organized societies of Northern Europe or the US. Now such small-scale, labour-intensive enterprise is becoming an option for a wider range of actors.[6]

The disappearance of stable industrial jobs in the West (and increasingly also in Asia as factories automate) and the transformation of the countryside in Africa and South America due to land grabbing and climate change, is pushing a generation of people out of traditional life forms. Many of them migrate, often not simply out of necessity but also because they feel that they deserve a better life for themselves and their families. Indeed, the dream of a better life has probably never been as widespread and tangible as it is now, as the features of a life lived with the latest iPhone in hand are visible on the cheap screens that have become ubiquitous even in the poorest of households. They try their luck in booming megacities that are unable to absorb them within an official labour market that is itself contracting. They attempt to make the hazardous journey into Europe, the US or some other part of the 'homeland' of industrial modernity. For most, an entrepreneurial solution remains the only viable alternative to slave-like labour conditions in textile sweat-shops or in the tomato fields of Southern Italy, or risky careers at the entry level of the criminal economy. For most, the aspiration is to set up your own business, to be your own man (or woman), to create a life that is a little better, a little more dignified and a little more meaningful.

The real novelty is that such popular industrious entrepreneurs are now increasingly joined by middle-class university graduates, who historically used to prefer stable employment to the vagaries of entrepreneurship. Such knowledge worker entrepreneurship is often a necessity. But it is also often a choice. To many, the bullshit nature of a corporate job becomes obvious after a few years and the aspiration is to do something else that is more fulfilling, creative or simply freer. To many, the ethical and existential imperative to change the world finds its expression in business and entrepreneurship. These tendencies will probably become even more pronounced in the future as automation and economic contraction combine to make corporate careers, whether middle-class or proletarian, even rarer to come by.

Capitalist restructuring has moved the industrious economy from the margins into the centre. Ever more the production of goods and services and, increasingly, innovation – at least of the adaptive, piecemeal variety – is relegated to small-scale labour-intensive companies. Already in the 1980s the automobile and electronics industry started to outsource component manufacturing to small labour-intensive factories, mostly located in what used to be the 'periphery' of the world economy. Corporate services followed suit. Today, the platform economy is creating new transport and delivery services organized in the form of a multitude of formally autonomous enterprises, often one-person operations, and the innovation needed to adapt digital technologies to new market niches is outsourced to thousands of start-ups.

However, the affirmation of the industrious sector is also due to the new commons that have resulted from the digitalization and globalization of capitalist production and culture, along with the affirmation of a number of alternatives like Free/Open Source Software or peer-production communities. These new commons make it easier and cheaper to organize complex business operations. Start-ups can be created on the cheap; cheap electronics can be imported and distributed on European and African popular markets though the complex coordination of a multitude of small-scale producers and intermediaries. Like the commons that supported the 'petty commodity producers' that built an emerging market society in the European Middle Ages, the new digital commons have substantially empowered contemporary industrious entrepreneurship. The industrious economy is not equipped to engage in genuinely disruptive innovation; it is not the place where nuclear fusion or quantum computing will come from. It is, however, very good, often better than the corporate giants that remain from the industrial age, to adapt existing technological solutions to popular needs and new market niches. It is perhaps possible that new commonly available technologies like blockchains and similar distributed ledgers, or plug-and-play software for data mining will render this small-scale industrious economy even more innovative in this sense. At the horizon we might see dodgy back-alley entrepreneurs churning out genetically modified tomato seeds fit to survive in the altered conditions of the Anthropocene.

The return of industrious relations of production, of petty commodity production albeit in a high-tech version, has been driven by capitalist restructuring. But it is also driving such restructuring. And it is already driving a substantial transformation in the nature of digital capitalism. Platform capitalism, the dominance of consumer-oriented platforms like Uber, Facebook or Amazon along with platform labour markets like Fiverr or 99designs can be understood as a strategy that aims at containing and controlling a multitude of small-scale enterprises by owning the markets that they operate on and taxing the transactions that they engage in. Indeed, since the 1980s, the institutional structure of today's platforms have evolved as a way of controlling extended corporate supply chains. Current plans for the industrial internet, or Industry 4.0, aim at extending such control by centralizing data gathered from a vast multitude of acts of production and consumption across national economies. As I will suggest later in the book, we might see an extension of this platform paradigm into a model of capitalism that combines mass entrepreneurship at the bottom, with top–down despotic control exercised via algorithms and big data.

However, industrious modernity also points beyond capitalism in important respects. Like the 'civic economy' of fourteenth-century Franciscans, today's petty producers imagine a decentralized market economy marked by transparency and relative equality – a world where economic action remains embedded in moral and civic responsibility; where 'value sovereignty' allows you to stay on the market while being true to your ethical aspirations. Whether and in what form such an industrious economy might survive remains an open question. It is, however, quite certain that the onset of the Anthropocene will accelerate the current crisis of industrial capitalism, just like the ecological crisis of the fourteenth century broke the backbone of feudalism. The accumulation of dysfunctionalities that will most likely mark the future of capitalism will open up new spaces for a decentralized industrious economy to affirm itself and grow more attractive as it addresses a large range of popular needs and provides the new forms of innovation needed, much like the crisis of feudalism in the fourteenth century provided a space in which the guilds and the commons-based market economy that they supported could grow. Maybe such a decentralized industrious economy might become capable of deploying state power in its own interest, maybe inventing radically new political forms along the way. Perhaps it will take the form of an informally regulated global bazaar economy operating out of the back alleys of the global planet of slums, building new life in the ruins. The latter might be the most likely scenario (and it seems the one towards which the intellectual pessimism of contemporary social theorists is converging).[7]

The return of industrious relations of production in a digitally empowered version is possibly the most important contradiction that marks contemporary capitalism, and it will be a crucial source of that system's future evolution or, perhaps, transformation. This book is an attempt to sketch out the emerging features of the contemporary condition of 'industrious modernity' and to speculate on its role in the coming transition, at least in the relatively short-run perspective of the immediate future of digital capitalism as we know it. The aim is not to promote a singular Great Idea, nor to offer any hope for future redemption, but rather to attempt a *realistic* sociological analysis of how contemporary developments might pan out.

The argument is divided into four chapters. The next chapter, 'The Crisis of Digital Capitalism', sets the stage and provides background (it also defines some basic concepts like 'capitalism'). The chapter deals with the present sense of stasis and our consequent inability to imagine a future that is different from the present. The premise here is that far from delivering a technological fix, digital technologies have been used to conserve the essential features of an industrial modernity in more or less permanent crisis. With this in mind, I have taken inspiration in the late Mark Fisher's essay on 'Capitalist Realism'. It succinctly spells out and dissects a condition where, as Frederic Jameson originally remarked, 'it is easier to imagine the end of the world than to see the end of capitalism'. My contribution rests with an attempt to understand why this is the case. How did the economic and social forces unleashed in the nineteenth-century Great Transformation subsequently turn in upon themselves to create a situation where, to once again use Mark Fisher's words, 'culture persists without the new' and even 'the young are no longer capable of producing surprises'?[8] How did digital technologies, once so pregnant with hopes of social and economic transformation, end up preserving, and sometimes reinforcing, the status quo? To make sense of this I present a (very short) story of the development, consolidation and crisis of industrial *capitalism*.

The development and successive decline of industrial capitalism has also generated two elements that are now pointing beyond it, towards a different kind of modernity. First, the 'real subsumption' of potentially all social relations, the networking and inclusion of life itself as a potential source of value within a 'bio-capitalism' that operates on a global scale, has realized new global commons in the form of skills, symbolic and cognitive resources and freely available technologies and platforms. These commons are ever more used in ways that evade or contrast with the logic of industrial capitalism. Second, the decline of industrial capitalism has created a growing reserve army of underemployed and highly skilled individuals who are using these new commons in order to realize a different kind of modernity, with their own life projects as well as with wider 'communities' in mind.

The long stasis of industrial capitalism has led to growing rates of passivity and depression. Mental illness and opiate addiction are both on the rise. Exclusion and lack of prospects feed the many millenarian movements driven by religious or political extremism that are proliferating in today's 'age of anger'.[9] At the same time, however, we are witnessing a new wave of entrepreneurial activity around the world, particularly among younger people for whom a start-up or a small business venture has become a possible response to a tighter labour market that offers fewer opportunities as well as to a social condition that offers little hope and few alternatives. Chapter 3, 'The Industrious Economy', provides an impressionistic survey of this multifaceted world: the start-ups and hipster businesses that proliferate in big cities; the small agricultural enterprises that mark the countryside of Southern Europe (as well as many Asian countries); the business archipelagos that have formed around Free or Open Source Software; blockchain technologies and other new digital commons; and the rise of the self-employed that has become a characteristic of Western labour markets. Alongside these, we have the dense networks of small-scale traders that constitute the 'pirate modernity' or 'globalization from below' that provide access to consumer goods to the poorer parts of the world's population that large capitalist companies have forgotten about long ago.

This industrious economy tends to be labour intensive and capital poor. Earnings tend to be low and motivations are wider than the strictly economic, like being creative, realizing oneself or simply finding a more dignified or less boring life. As Braudel pointed out, this economy is located in the middle, in between the Great Exchange of financial capital and the *longue durée* of everyday life – between the power of capital and the drudgery of labour. This middle layer is populated by downwardly mobile knowledge workers unable to reproduce the privileged class position of their parents, and of upwardly mobile people from popular backgrounds, like the urban migrant who puts up a cell phone repair store and becomes an employer. Whether privileged or proletarian in origin, these actors are converging into a new middle class or petty bourgeoisie, which is becoming the carrying stratum of a new industrious modernity. Increasingly they have come to share a similar world view and material condition.

But the industrious economy is also in the middle in the sense of being in the midst of life. Industrious modernity is an expression of an economic reality that remains embedded in social relations, where economic rationality is not completely separated from the value rationality of everyday life. This can be a matter of traditional value horizons, however revamped, as in the case of the Senegalese traders who peddle knock-off bags on the streets of Southern Europe while acting as part of a transnational community held together by common faith and with strong communitarian obligations. It can be a matter of communities constructed anew, as in the case of the many co-working spaces that work hard to make members feel part of something grander and more meaningful, or the many blockchain ventures that take the form of co-living experiments, combining work with affective and relational life.

The diverse expressions of this industrious economy are converging around a common economic ethic, marked by a common emphasis on the need or even obligation to change the world through enterprise. I suggest that the story behind this is more complex than what common references to an all-pervasive neoliberal ideology might suggest. True, entrepreneurship has become a new pop-cultural icon by means of numerous television shows and self-help manuals of the Oprah Winfrey variety. It has also been inculcated in the younger generation by means of a thorough socialization in the realities of neoliberal existence, where you are made to think of yourself as an entrepreneur who is inclined to take risks and maximize the value of one's assets. But entrepreneurship is not simply something that is hammered into the heads of the young by teachers, social workers and career counsellors. It is also something that is embraced by a large number of people, a far larger number, arguably, than those who still engage in politics in the classic, twentieth-century sense of the term. For these people, entrepreneurship is not simply an economic activity. It also comes with a vision of social transformation. For some, this is simply a matter of improving their own lives or those of their family or friends. For many, however, entrepreneurship remains the only viable way to 'change the world' or 'make a difference'. Entrepreneurship has become the perhaps most widespread manifestation of what Hannah Arendt called 'action', the civic activity that ever since Aristotle has distinguished 'man' as a political animal. It has taken over from politics as the main field in which such action can unfold in the pragmatic everyday of 'actually doing something'. At the very least, it has become a way to acquire what sociologist Anthony Giddens has called 'ontological security', a sense that one's life has meaning and makes sense.[10]

Indeed, today's industrious modernity is very similar to the modernity brought forth by Weber's Protestants. Like today's industrious entrepreneurs, the members of seventeenth-century puritan sects were cast out or had fled a collapsing feudal society. Like today's industrious entrepreneurs, they found themselves in an expanding market society for which there was no direction, no historical precedent. Like today, they invented the idea of work as a calling as a way to make sense of this condition. (As we shall see, this idea has antecedents that go further back, at least to the millennial movements of the eleventh century that rose out of the first contradictions of feudalism.) Indeed, there is a clear genealogy that connects key elements of the contemporary industrious ethic, like in the notion of work as guided by some sort of 'calling' or the doctrine of 'disruptive innovation' to the magical thinking of, in particular, American Protestantism.

Chapter 4, 'Industrious Capitalism', takes a closer look at how the conditions for the contemporary industrious economy have emerged out of the last decades of 'post-Fordist' restructuring. In particular, I point at the rise of an 'immaterial' service economy, the globalization of production (both material and immaterial; in fact the two tend to converge in the digital economy) and the growth of new planetary commons. The chapter goes on to examine the capitalist responses to the industriousness that results from these developments, in the form of the start-up/venture capital system and its product, an economy of platform 'unicorns'. The conclusion is that far from realizing the full potential of the digital technologies that stand at the heart of the new industriousness, the current capitalist response tends to stand-ardize innovation and stifle economic growth. Overall, it is a conservative response, not particularly suited to valorizing the potential of the new relations of production that have been unleashed by digital connectivity. (My contribution to contem-porary debates on 'digital labour' would thus be to suggest that the main problem is not that Facebook exploits its users, but that it does not exploit them very efficiently.) Possibly a Chinese cycle of accumulation, combining mass entrepre-neurship and platform governance with a coherent strategy for social and economic development might prove a more efficient solution, at least in the short run. The chapter ends by examining the social and economic models that are emerging from the industrious economy itself: from experiments in platform cooperatives, via new guild-like organizations and peer-production projects. The survey suggests that rather than alternatives to markets and exchange (as many of the more ideologically conscious of these alternatives claim to be), the cooperative or 'commonist' part of the industrious economy instead promotes a new kind of civic economy where small-scale market exchange is embedded in communitarian values. Similar to early modern notions of a civic economy, proponents of *commonism* imagine a society built on simple commodity exchange between roughly egalitarian actors who remain true to their value horizons. To date, few of these initiatives are able to sustain themselves economically (with the exception, perhaps, of the alternative food economy). Most remain dependent on the 'true' capitalist economy or on state funding in some form. However, technological and institutional innovation is proceeding and already in 2018, the world of blockchain ventures has managed to create a substantial autonomous circuit of venture capital. Whether or not this crypto-economy is sustainable, it represents a tangible alternative to the official venture capital system: a non-capitalist market for capital, in effect.

Overall, this is not an optimistic book. Unlike influential thinkers like Paul Mason or Jeremy Rifkin, I do not suggest that the present developments in the digital economy will make us stumble, almost inadvertently, into communism. Nor do I think that the contemporary crisis – of capitalism or of the environment – will kick new life into old social movements and that these will somehow take over and take control, bringing us back to the safety and direction of industrial modernity once again.[11] In the final chapter, 'A New Industrious Revolution?', I will instead propose that the decline of feudalism can offer an alternative historical parallel with which to make sense of the present situation. In the social sciences, as well as in radical politics, we are used to modelling our ideas on the events of the eighteenth and nineteenth centuries and we are used to thinking of social change as revolutionary. In many ways, however, our times look more like the fourteenth century. Capitalism is going through a period of what I call 're-feudalization', where it is becoming less able to valorize the productive potential that it has realized. This leads to growing polarization of wealth and higher levels of exploitation. The serfs of yesteryear fled the countryside or were pushed out by processes of enclosure and land reclamations. In the cities they engaged in industrious commercial activity using common skills and resources. They went on to form guilds and corporations that not only protected them from market fluctuations, but also provided new common resources and a new sense of identity and purpose. These institutions and the new life-forms that they supported grew to become an increasingly attractive alternative as the crisis of feudalism deepened. The environmental disasters of the fourteenth century brought that crisis to bear and essentially broke the backbone of the old feudal order. What followed was a period of conflicts, wars and rebellions, as well as new possibilities. Religious and social movements proliferated and new economic and political models emerged. Gradually a new politics took shape, which was able to usher in modernity as we have come to know it. Beneath these grand events there was the *longue durée* of purposeful, sometimes passionate, labour-intensive enterprise, of what contemporary economic historians (mostly referring to the later period of the seventeenth and eighteenth centuries) have come to call an 'industrious revolution'. Industriousness, however, is not revolutionary; it is a matter of incremental piecemeal change that takes place within a social model that appears to be unaltered at the surface, until it bursts through in the spectacular events that we associate with the origins of modernity.

In early modern Europe, capitalism could eventually break through and reshape the world in its image. This 'Great Divergence' by means of which capitalist Europe took off on a spectacular trajectory of economic growth and world conquest depended on a number of conditions – interstate competition that allowed capitalist interests to expand, a new energy paradigm, a world open to colonization and conquest – most of which are not present today. Above all, there is no 'spatial fix', no further expansion that can solve the present crisis and allow capitalist accumulation to go on. This points at a fundamental difference in relation to the European early modern experience; rather than evolving, capitalism is likely to become increasingly conservative and, for a variety of reasons, less relevant to a growing number of people. It looks like the system might contract, rather than expand. The likely outcome is a gradual but accelerating collapse, as systemic dysfunctionalities, ecological disasters and increasing costs related to resource scarcity overlap. In this drawn-out period of systemic collapse, industrious modernity might provide the blueprint for a different social model, able to survive, and perhaps even prosper, in the 'capitalist ruins' left behind.

2

The Crisis of Digital Capitalism

In 1987, Robert Solow, the Nobel laureate economist, famously claimed that 'we can see computers everywhere, except in the productivity statistics'. Today we can say similar things about digital technologies. We see them everywhere, in the home, at work and on the metro where people travel 'alone together', each staring into their little screens, in the spooky surveillance algorithms that track our everyday life, and in the new magic world of bitcoin. The spread of digital technologies has been so fast that in only two decades since the invention of the user-friendly internet, almost half of the world's population have come to use them on a regular basis. But digital technologies do not seem to be able to generate enough economic growth to live up to the grandiose expectations that accompanied their arrival, or even to secure a decent standard of living for the growing global workforce. So far, they have not created an open-ended, participatory economy where monopolies have been eroded by the competition from a multitude of small actors and where the new gains resulting from cheaper production and easier transactions have benefitted all.[1] While the last two decades have lifted more than one billion people out of destitute poverty, this has mainly been a matter of (mostly Chinese) rural masses entering into the modern economy. For those who were already there, and in particular for the younger generations that are entering the system now, things look less rosy. For middle-class university graduates, the chances of making a comfortable living out of a steady career, to buy a house and a car, have kids and go on holiday like the baby boomers did, have become much slimmer. Even as university tuition fees have gone up massively, it is no longer certain that a degree, however expensive, will automatically translate into a corporate job that, however soulless, will at least pay the bills and provide for retirement. And even if you manage to enter the game, careers are much less stable and work is much more consuming than what it used to be. For most, insecurity and precarity is becoming the norm. The situation is less destitute in high-growth countries like India and China, but even there, the great increase in university graduates is in the process of creating massive graduate unemployment. Already now the problem of young educated middle-class men (in particular) who spend their lives 'waiting' for professional life and adulthood to begin has become a significant issue. For the popular classes, most paths to upward social mobility have in effect been shut down. The choice is between low-paid labour-intensive forms of iSlavery in the factories of the South or the Amazon warehouses of the North and an expanding informal or criminal economy. Inclusive economic development, the (in)famous trickling down of wealth and rising up of talent that the implicit 'social contract' of industrial society was based on is now a thing of the past. Instead, we have a growing polarization between the increasingly wealthy 1 per cent (or 0.1 per cent) and the denizens of the 'planet of slums' that sprawls around the gentrified city centres where they dwell.[2]

What is perhaps even more serious is that digital capitalism seems unable to face the challenges that come with the massive transformation of the planetary environment that is now underway. Global warming, ocean acidification and species extinction, to name just a few processes, will threaten the very basis of our contemporary 'lifestyle' and pose a serious challenge to the survival of global civilization as we know it. Even so, the powers that be seem unable to act and address the issue, but remain locked into their destructive paths. As Naomi Klein points out, actions to mitigate climate change appear to be diametrically opposed to the short-run interest of established capitalist elites.[3] Everyday existence, particularly for the young, is ever more focused on the present, in a condition of Capitalist Realism, where, as Mark Fisher writes: 'For most people under twenty in Europe and North America, the lack of alternatives to capitalism is no longer even an issue. Capitalism has seamlessly occupied the horizons of the thinkable.' Everyday life is lived in a state of 'depressive hedonism', where the void of a meaningless existence is filled up with 'hedonic lassitude' – the easily available micro pleasures of YouTube, fast food, social media and PlayStation. Any real change seems impossible. It has become easier for us to imagine the end of the world than to see the end of the contemporary arrangements that we know as (post)industrial capitalism, to paraphrase a famous Marxist thinker, and we no longer mean that hypothetically. The end of the world – as we know it – now seems quite real.[4]

Why is this so? Why can't we just 'change the world', or even, like the revolutionaries of the last turn of the century, dream about doing so? That is not an easy question to answer. To make a serious attempt, we have to take a closer look at the nature of the digital capitalism that we have come to live in.

Capitalism

What is capitalism? Some say that capitalism is the same as a free market economy, distinguishing it from the planned economies that marked what used to be known as the 'actually existing socialism' of the Soviet Union and the 'Eastern Bloc'. Indeed, a central claim of recent neoliberal policies has been that the capitalist economy would gain from advancing free markets as opposed to state intervention. However, in reality it is not that simple. In the nineteenth century, when most of the theories of capitalism that we use were originally formulated, it was quite straightforward to equate capitalism with free markets. This was a time when capitalism advanced through the expansion of markets, breaking down the old monopolies and privileges of the *ancien régime*, and opening up economies for competition and meritocracy. The English industrial revolution that provided the context for Marx's analysis of capitalism was based on relatively small companies (by today's measures) who engaged in intense competition, and suffered the Dickensian vagaries of fluctuating business cycles.[5] With this example in mind, it is easy to equate capitalism with markets, a view that has become even more plausible by recent decades of neoliberal reforms whereby marketization has invested in public services as well as growing areas of everyday practice, from eating to finding romantic partners.[6] At the same time, contemporary capitalism is mostly organized around large and powerful corporations and financial actors and, lately, platform unicorns like Uber or Amazon. They do not rely on markets as much as they rely on planning. A contemporary global company like Apple or Fiat is a complex web of contracts, obligations, management routines and algorithmic control systems that can involve thousands of units and small firms, and maybe millions of individuals. It is, in effect, a planned economy where actions are guided by adminis-trative routines, not by individual utility maximization on the market. Indeed, these large companies seek to avoid engaging in market competition as much as possible. Instead, they try to sit on and own particular markets. As Peter Thiel, co-founder of PayPal, early investor in Facebook and partner in the $2 billion venture capital firm Founders Fund explained in his *Wall Street Journal* article, 'Competition is for losers':

> Americans mythologize competition and credit it with saving us from socialist bread lines. Actually, capitalism and competition are opposites. Capitalism is premised on the accumulation of capital, but under perfect competition, all profits get competed away. The lesson for entrepreneurs is clear: If you want to create and capture lasting value, don't build an undifferentiated commodity business.[7]

In this situation, a Braudelian perspective is more plausible. To the French historian Fernand Braudel, capitalism is not the same thing as markets. Instead, he views capitalism as a system that developed historically through attempts to control and regulate markets on the part of small cliques of powerful interests, like the Venetian and Genoese traders who fought over the control of trading routes in the fourteenth century, the large agricultural entrepreneurs that took control over the wool trade in England or the Florentine and Genoese bankers who managed to take control of and shape the European financial economy during the fourteenth and fifteenth centuries. Markets, on the other hand, are well-nigh universal in recorded history, going back at least as far as the origins of urban civilization. Capitalism is more recent, and is usually imposed 'from above' in some way, mostly via the exercise of state power.[8] Sometimes this advance of capitalism happens through the creation of new markets. Sometimes it happens instead through the monopolization of markets. Indeed, rather than markets and exchange, it is easier to understand capitalism as a particular system of production and consumption, as a kind of social metabolism, if you will.

Capitalism is a very particular social arrangement where the production of useful things is subordinated to the imperative to make a profit. The contemporary world economy churns out an unprecedented number of cars, iPhones, toasters and other stuff. But it does so as a consequence of the overall imperative to make money that can be reinvested to make even more money in the future, not the other way around. True, there have always been people interested in making a profit. But to arrange whole societies this way is historically unique, to Northwest Europe and the US since the second half of the nineteenth century, and to the whole planet since the 1990s, more or less.

Capitalism is older than the industrial version that we have come to know. Already in late medieval Europe there emerged a consolidated network of wealthy merchants united by a common interest in expanding their wealth and resources. This capitalist *class* was able to exercise substantial political influence, mainly by financing wars in exchange for trade monopolies. They also provided most of the energy behind the commercialization of agriculture and the enclosure and privatization of the common lands that, much like what is happening in parts of Africa and South America today, drove growing numbers of European peasants into the expanding cities. These early capitalists pushed for the opening up of new trade routes, forming companies with state participation, like the famous East India Companies, which provided military support to help European merchants impose their terms of trade in Asia, and then went on to form privately owned colonies. In the Atlantic these merchant networks transformed pristine islands like Madeira or Jamaica into plantation colonies and enslaved millions to mass-produce sugar or cotton for the expanding European market. But apart from the people who were enslaved or colonized, this early capitalism did not transform everyday life for the masses. For most of the European population, as well as for the some 300 million who lived in eighteenth-century China, it was but a distant rumble. The real change, the true Great Transformation, came with industrialization.[9]

Industrialization institutionalized a number of systemic exchanges – Marx called them 'metabolic' exchanges – with the life processes, human and non-human, in its surroundings. This made life co-dependent on the process of industrial production and capital accumulation and successively altered life as it is lived to fit the model. Industrialization represented the beginning of the fusion between capitalism and life, what some now refer to as 'bio-capitalism'.[10]

The first of these metabolic exchanges involved human life processes in industrial production. The factory was the fundamental novelty of the nineteenth century, although there had been precedents in plantations, army barracks and manufacturers centuries earlier. Its novelty was that the business of making things no longer followed traditional patterns but was organized by the mechanical rhythm of factory machinery. Workers were progressively de-skilled; what counted was no longer their ability to craft things, but their ability to do what they were told and to follow the job description. Similarly, the time of work no longer followed the old human rhythm where work and life were intermixed, where conversation and banter went on while working in the fields or spinning at home, and work itself followed the natural rhythms of the day, starting at dawn and ending at dusk. Instead, the factory system demanded that workers present themselves at a fixed time and then work efficiently and in silence for a fixed number of hours. The factory system aimed at transforming workers into cogs in a machinery able to dispense measurable and comparable units of 'abstract labour' during the day.[11]

What was not work became leisure – to engage in one's free time – and soon it was to undergo a similar process of organization. The new mass communications, the cheap 'penny press' in the nineteenth century and radio, television, film and music in the twentieth, quickly became part of the new culture industries spreading new leisure habits and lifestyles and paving the way for the branding of industrially produced consumer goods. This rapidly replaced a traditional popular culture with an industrially organized culture centred on consumer goods, to fit the new urban environment. The seductive organization of leisure centred on the pleasures of television shows, fast fashions and microwavable ready meals was supported by new and more efficient forms of discipline and surveillance. Compulsory schooling taught people to sit still and accept authority. A functioning police force made breaking the law much riskier than before. The regulation of public behaviour effectively diminished levels of violence and crime, criminalized some forms of deviant behaviour and regulated others. All of this contributed to the creation of modern populations that were both more orderly and more predictable. In the last decade this process has culminated in the spread of social media that have penetrated the everyday life rhythms of billions of people and made their social interaction, entertainment and distraction unfold on digital platforms, where new data are generated that serve, in turn, to refine the placement and branding of consumer goods and, through surveillance and data mining, render actions ever more predictable.[12]

There was continuous resistance to this process of metabolic inclusion – from the machine-breaking movements of the nineteenth century to the countercultures of the twentieth, including parts of the labour movement – but industrial capitalism proved extraordinarily capable of learning from its antagonists and incorporating their ideas into new innovations, transforming in effect resistance into a resource for further expansion. The result is that, by the end of the twentieth century human life across the planet, with few exceptions, is lived within the metabolic machinery of industrial capitalism. It feeds off industrially produced goods – from food to clothes, housing and entertainment – and most of its conscious existence is dedicated to producing such goods, either creating them materially in factories, reproducing the lifestyles that give them meaning and value or organizing the ever more complex interlinkages between the material and immaterial aspects of capital accumulation.

The second great metabolic exchange was institutionalized between industrial capitalism and non-human life forms. Human life has transformed its non-human environment ever since the emergence of settled agricultural communities in the Neolithic (some say ever since the invention of fire some 400,000 years ago). Domesticating animals, selectively breeding crops, cutting down forests and growing new germs in the close interaction between humans and domesticated animals, humans have been an important 'force of nature' throughout their known history. However, their impact accelerated massively with industrialization. First, because industrialization was based on a new energy paradigm: fossilized carbon, in the form of coal, and oil and gas, instead of animal and human muscles, wind and water. This was a decisive factor. Most of the basic ideas behind industrial production were present already in the early eighteenth century, but it was not until the commercialization of steam engines that they could be put into practice. Similarly, the absence of great coal reserves was one important reason why eighteenth-century China, where levels of technical and commercial sophistication rivalled those of Europe, did not embark on the path of industrialization. Second, the global spread of industrial modernity in its great take-off in the second part of the twentieth century was premised on the systematic transformation of agriculture. Synthetic fertilizers, pesticides and the massive mechanization of agriculture transformed food production worldwide, from the predominance of small, family-based farms using traditional methods to the dominance of large monoculture crops. This massively increased efficiency, reducing the cost of calories, but it also greatly reduced bio-diversity. The combination of these two factors – cheap energy and cheap food – contributed to the massive expansion of the human population and its concentration within growing cities where people were forced to – more or less successfully – make do within the context of an industrial lifestyle, selling their skills and labour in order to buy necessities or luxuries made by strangers in anonymous factories. This growing population had no alternative but to live in symbiosis with industrial capitalism, whether they liked it or not.[13]

Industrial capitalism

By the second half of the twentieth century these metabolic exchanges were institutionalized in a social model that we have come to know as industrial capitalism (or industrial society). Simply put, this industrial model was based on capital-intensive manufacturing: large factories using expensive machines to produce lots of stuff cheaper than before (relying on what economists call 'economies of scale'). It was organized around a strict division of labour between cognitive and manual work. A small managerial elite drew up the plans, designed the goods and organized the processes of production as well as of consumption, and a large mass of manual workers or ordinary consumers simply followed suit, executing the job description as provided and desiring the stuff they saw on TV. Along with this came a welfare system, public or corporate, that guaranteed stability, insured against sickness and old age, and made sure that the labour force was disciplined, appropriately skilled and could be counted on to support the system and give it legitimacy. While this 'ideal typical' model was never fully implemented in reality, it acted as a guiding reference for processes of modernization across the world, in the North as well as in the South, communist or 'free'. For a time virtually everyone thought that substituting big factories for small business, salaried work for self-employment and regulated modern existence for 'traditional' or unruly bohemian forms of life, was a good idea.[14]

Industrial modernity permitted a massive expansion of the human population on the planet. For most people it also meant a better life: people today tend to be better fed, live longer, have more stuff at their disposal and be better informed compared to in the eighteenth century. However, this process has also massively expanded the processes of capitalist metabolism, as the unfolding of industrial modernity has come to require enormous amounts of new resources. In this way processes that used to be outside the reach of capital accumulation, like the lives of thousands of non-human species, oceanic ecosystems and even the climate itself, have been included into this symbiosis and profoundly transformed by it.

Importantly, the metabolic expansion of industrial modernity provided a space for the sustained growth of the capitalist economy. Capitalism is a system that has continuous growth in its DNA, so to say. Individual capitalists need to expand, or they are eaten up by someone else who expands. The system as a whole is oriented towards the creation of profits, gains and earnings that were not there to start with. Profits are invested to expand the productive forces, and new markets need to be opened up that can absorb what these new productive forces can produce. Transforming a country of peasants into a country of workers and consumers, over a lifetime in England, over two to three lifetimes in the rest of Europe and over two decades in China, provided space for such expansion. Connecting three million people to the internet and providing half of them with a smartphone did a similar trick more recently. Now, however, that expansion seems to have stalled.

Some would say that this is because capitalism by now has, in effect, consumed the planet. We are running out of the crucial resources, oil, land, rare metals, and perhaps soon enough food and water, which feed the system and there is simply no other place to go. But people have said this in the past, many times, and each time they have been proven wrong. Adam Smith, for example, imagined market-driven economic development to transform the whole world into a prosperous version of Scotland or the Netherlands. He certainly did not foresee the sixteen-fold rise in standards of living that would result from the industrial revolution that was taking off right under his nose. Similarly, for us it is impossible to imagine what kinds of new wealth can come out of new energy systems and more rational forms of resource utilization and ecological stewardship. The point is that contemporary capitalism does not seem to be able to make this happen. Why?[15]

Capitalism is both revolutionary and conservative. Industrial capitalism remade the planet and the life we live on it in ways that might have been more radical than anything ever experienced in human history. It did so by furthering a particular form of social organization: industrial mass production for mass consumption. In order to do this a lot of resources had to be invested in structures that remain difficult to change: building productive facilities, factories and distribution networks, creating an infrastructure (highways, petrol stations and electricity grids) and creating lifestyles (the nuclear family, suburban living) and social institutions (participatory democracy, the welfare state) to sustain it. And for some time it worked. Economic growth created new jobs that were better paid. People who were used to tougher circumstances could get those jobs and use their new resources to buy into the new comforts available. Their consumption created demand for new goods, and sustained popular consensus for the social model. It might not have been perfect, but it was better than what earlier generations had and, importantly, there was hope that the next generation would have it even better.

Then, gradually at first, this space for expansion narrowed. It became more difficult to sell cars or washing machines because most people who could afford them already had them. The skills and know-how necessary to make these things had become more widely available, and as the companies who had made money making cars or washing machines invested their profits in new markets, capital became more easily available as well. New producers started to compete for what was left of the market, often offering the same goods at lower prices, something they could do if they were based in places that had not reached the same level of industrialization, like Japan in the 1970s, Korea in the 1980s or China in the 1990s and 2000s. Prices went down, competition grew stiffer and profit margins shrank. At the same time, people who already had cars and refrigerators wanted more out of life. A new generation of workers were no longer content with the 'standard package' of mass consumption; they wanted more equal and democratic arrangements and they went on strike. Middle-class youth went to university: now they desired self-realization and meaningful lives. In short, life as a capitalist became more difficult. But the present arrangement is not that easy to change. Millions of people make a living from it and powerful interests get rich from it. Above all, the mobilization of pleasures and desires creates a limit to the imagination. It becomes very difficult to imagine a life that is lived in any other way. 'Capitalist realism' – the impossibility to envision an alternative – is not only a feature of the contemporary 'neoliberal' epoch that Mark Fisher writes about. At the very least, it has been with us since at least the post-war years, when consumer culture won over older ideological visions and overcame traditional life forms on a massive scale.

The scenario above was essentially what happened in the 1970s in the West. New global competition combined with increasing worker resistance and the fact that the then leading power, the US, was losing its ability to police the global order it had created (failing to prevent the OPEC countries from raising the price of oil by 25 per cent in 1973, for example), led to a steady decline in industrial profitability.[16] At the time, there were many voices that championed an overall systemic change. More radical parts of the workers' movement saw times as ripe for revolution. A younger generation of knowledge workers was experimenting with alternative lifestyles, politically inclined as well as more spiritually oriented, leading to new countercultures that spanned the spectrum from violent political protest to new-age self-realization. There were attempts at developing alternative energy forms, championing local production systems and developing lifestyles that did not involve mass consumption. Many of these saw new digital technologies as an important tool for creating such alternative arrangements. Intel had invented the microchip in 1971 and the internet was in its infancy, the first connection on Arpanet, its predecessor, having been made in 1969. Stewart Brand, later to found *Wired* magazine and become a chief spokesperson for the 'Californian ideology' of Silicon Valley in the 1970s, built a business selling assembly kits for personal computers along with beads and other hippie-wear to the movement of alternative communes that grew in the US.[17]

Digital capitalism

But digital technologies also proved useful in perpetuating the basic features of the industrial model. This was indeed what happened in the 1970s. The combination of computer-aided design and computer-aided manufacturing (CAD/CAM for those familiar with the technology) and early digital communication systems like corporate internets allowed companies to relocate production away from large factories to growing networks of small factories, first in their vicinity but gradually spreading across the globe. This outsourcing, and later globalization, of production reduced the power of the industrial working class (what's the point in striking if there is no place to strike in?). It also reduced the cost of producing basic commodities, as production could be relegated to small companies with lower profit margins and often employing workers who were paid substantially lower wages and were less organized than the Western working class.[18] It did open up new consumer markets as new workers, however dismal their pay, desired and could afford at least some industrially produced commodities. But it also led to new levels of capital concentration. Not everyone could globalize production: this required substantial investments in information systems and other managerial resources; it required an army of managers to implement the new organization. And for those who did, competing on global markets where the technical and aesthetic features of goods were increasingly similar required substantial investments in innovation, flexibility, brands and other so-called 'intangible assets'. These, and in particular global brand building, were costly and demanded substantial amounts of capital to be invested in communication, advertising and real estate to secure a global presence. (Italian fashion brands, for example, became heavily indebted in the 1990s as they invested massively in global branding, buying advertising time on television networks across the world and securing physical presence, with stores in exclusive shopping centres from Shanghai to Rio.) This meant that only the largest and the most powerful actors survived. Indeed, digital capitalism has been marked by a substantial process of capital concentration across virtually all sectors, where the share of profits that go to the largest actors as well as their productivity levels has increased across the board. The internet, to take the most obvious example, began as an open system that, like radio in the 1920s, allowed a multitude of new small actors to find their niche. In just two decades, it has been substantially monopolized by the Big Five: Google, Facebook, Microsoft, Amazon and Apple. Similar things have happened to most manufacturing industries, from cars to computer chips, as well as branches of the culture industries like publishing, film or music.[19]

An additional and related factor that has contributed to such processes of capital concentration has been the growing importance of finance as a source of corporate profits. Throughout its history, capitalism has traditionally oscillated between periods of expansion based on the production and sale of commodities, and periods where instead profits were made mostly on financial markets. Generally, such periods of financialization have signalled the end of a 'cycle of accumulation', or, in other words, that a particular idea for how to grow and make money has exhausted its potential. This is precisely what began to happen in the 1970s as declining profits from the production and sale of commodities meant that large multinationals became more interested in investing on financial markets or inventing new kinds of financial services, where profit margins were higher, at least in the short run, and where higher liquidity insured against market risks that followed from a more volatile environment. Today, such traditional forms of financialization have been further enforced by the new productive arrangements developed by digital capitalism itself. First, the globalization of production has increased competition between producers at the bottom of global value chains and reduced the profit margins from manufacturing. The growing number of actors involved in production as well as, notably, logistics (a sector that has expanded rapidly with globalization) has created many more opportunities for financial gains. The more actors that are involved in productive processes, the more insecurities emerge within the system (Will my client deliver on time? Will they pay on time? Will the shipment arrive on time?). Financial actors can transform these into calculable estimates of risk, that can be sold on as financial instruments, like insurance.

At the same time, declining welfare states and increasing precarity and occupational insecurity has meant that life itself becomes more insecure. Here, too, financial markets have stepped in to offer private insurance and various forms of loans and credit, for education, for housing, for consumption. This has radically increased the level of household indebtedness in advanced economies, and made everyday life ever more dependent on the vagaries of financial markets (what will the interest rate on my mortgage be? What will my pension, invested in the stock market, be?). Digital technologies themselves have created much more efficient instruments for financial trading, from computerized trading terminals and quantitative hedge funds using data mining algorithms, to the proliferation of trading bots that we see today, automatically executing trading strategies by the millisecond.[20] However, once again, finance, and in particular high finance is not for everyone. To gain entry and to acquire the necessary technologies and information systems require substantial investments. Most importantly, corporations realize financial gains by capitalizing on their market power. Very simply, an automobile company with thousands of smaller factories in their supply chain can use their market power to impose different interest rates and terms of payment in their supply chain. They can access liquid resources for themselves at almost zero cost. They can then lend these to their suppliers at substantially higher interest rates and at the same time sell them insurance against risks posed by *their* suppliers. They pay their suppliers after ninety days, but require their retailers to anticipate the cost for new cars before they are sold to the public. In this way large automobile companies, like other large corporations, make most of their money from their financial activity, and not from actually making and selling cars. This is more like an excuse for acting like a bank. The growing importance of financial activity has meant that corporate earnings increasingly take the form of rent, the ability to control and tax productive processes that one does not necessarily intervene in. In the 1950s, corporate income deriving from financial activities was negligible; today it stands at around 40 per cent of earnings for large firms.[21] Indeed, the intangible assets that account for most of contemporary industrial productivity, as well as for a growth share of market valuations of big firms, essentially represent the ability to exercise such power over markets and supply chains. They are subsequently evaluated on financial markets where their capacity to guarantee future rent extraction is estimated.

This tends to reinforce the conservative nature of large corporations. If earnings come from the ability to build and protect market power, rather than from the ability to innovate and compete – 'competition is for losers' as Peter Theil suggested – then it is rational to use resources to protect such market power to the fullest. In this way corporations tend to invest in measures to preserve their market power. This means that they tend to be less inclined to take the kinds of risks that come with innovation and developing new products. If you already dominate the smartphone market, why do something else? This conservative nature has been further reinforced by the predominance of what is known as shareholder-oriented corporate governance. Managers, and in particular top managers, are obliged to act in the interest of the people who have a financial stake in the company as a rent-generating machine. Often top managers are among those people, as their bonuses are related to the financial performance of companies. This leads to favouring short-term gains, often constructed artificially by cutting short-term costs or even 'cooking the books' over long-term investments. It tends to further decrease the willingness to experiment or take risks.

The re-feudalization of capital

Capitalism has embarked on a retreat from productive activities. Across the world, assets are increasingly concentrated in a handful of large companies, and less of these assets are invested in actually making things. In the last decades, aspects of commodity production, starting with simple menial tasks and moving on to encompass more complicated things like innovation, design and product development, has been outsourced to small, capital-poor actors. Innovation is outsourced to small start-up companies, while at the same time, investments in overall R&D are declining (at least in the

US; China shows a different picture). It has come to the point where many scholars now suggest that industrial capitalism has lost its ability to sustain continuous innovation, and recent studies show a sustained decline in the productivity of the money that is spent on research.[22] At the same time, large corporations are awash with cash. The cash reserves of the US corporate sector are at record levels. As of 2018, Apple alone sits on more than $200 billion in cash reserves, not to speak of platform giants like Facebook or Google. Apart from lavish salaries or extravagant corporate 'campuses', this money is used to buy up other companies, either through mergers and acquisitions or on the private equity markets where there is no transparency and where valuations often remain unsubstantiated. (Why was Instagram worth $19 billion when Facebook bought it in in 2013? Why is Uber worth more than $60 billion today when the company keeps losing money and has no sustainable business model?[23]) It is as if the capitalists of this world have abandoned the game of actually making and selling stuff, much less innovating new stuff, to retreat into their own private parlour games where they keep buying and selling one another's companies, or at the most, dreaming up grandiose philanthropic projects to 'change the world'. Capitalism is becoming ever more similar to the feudalism that preceded it, a society that, particularly in its final phase, was marked by seigneurial conflicts and courtly intrigues, for which ordinary people mattered very little.

Indeed, contemporary capitalism looks a lot like the Italian fifteenth century when the expansion of the great merchant cities began to slow down, and when commercial cooperation was increasingly replaced by inter-capitalist competition and warfare. True this 'war of all against all' as Jacob Burckhardt called it, produced the Renaissance, along with a spectacular rise in conspicuous luxury consumption. But it was also the beginning of the end of the centrality of the Italian 'world economy' and a harbinger of a move of the gravitational centre of European capitalism towards the Northwest. While wealthy merchants who abandoned risky market activity for investment in landed property and sponsorship of the arts contributed to the creation of much beauty and refinement, the Italian economy never recovered.[24] Similar processes of re-feudalization, where capital retreats from risky market activity to instead invest in landed property or other safe assets and engage in luxury consumption, is a feature of the last phase of each cycle of accumulation in the history of capitalism. In fifteenth-century Florence as well as in eighteenth-century Amsterdam, it created a wealth of artistic and cultural riches. (Today it seems more oriented to the new standard package of luxury consumption visible through Instagram-hashtags like #richkidsofdubai.) In each case capitalism, in its re-feudalizing phase, tends to support ideas and social visions that are less interested in imagining a future and less able to imagine an alternative to the present. It is enough to compare the 'humanist' thinkers of the Italian thirteenth and fourteenth centuries who imagined a better future where markets and trade would go hand in hand with freedom, individualism and greater democracy, to Machiavelli, the great Renaissance political thinker, who instead proposed a realist (some would say cynical) political vision that reflected the increasingly polarized and conflictual reality of a Florence in economic decline. For him there was no future, but the endless game of struggle for power and hegemony.[25] Similarly today, large corporations are unable to think beyond the cynical game of defending and consolidating market position; at the most they imagine more of the same (iPhone X anyone?). They sit on enormous cash reserves but do not know how to use them, apart from paying themselves and their top managers huge dividends. Their advisors tell us, like Jordan Peterson, to find the answers to precarity and economic decline within ourselves. The alternative is dystopic visons of the end of civilization or religious fantasies about 'the singularity'. The most advanced capitalist prophet that we have, Elon Musk, proposes, like a contemporary Marie Antoinette, that if we cannot live on Earth we could go to Mars.

This is not simply a problem for us, the 99 per cent, but for capitalism itself. Without visions, new markets and productive investment, capitalism has entered a terminal crisis. Slower growth leads to higher unemployment and lower wages, which further reduces demand and creates a vicious circle. People who do not get anything out of the system are less inclined to support it and pay taxes. The state is left with fewer resources to ensure the reproduction of labour power via schooling, pensions and health care. This leads to an accumulation of inefficiencies. Capitalism, in its industrial version, can only provide a 'long and painful period of cumulative decay: of intensifying frictions, of fragility and uncertainty', to use German sociologist Wolfgang Streeck's words, and it is increasingly becoming an obstacle to progress that nobody has the strength to move out of the way. The future of capitalism appears to be fizzling out. It is becoming a system that is relevant to a decreasing part of the world population: a small managerial elite who live in gentrified city centres and consume ever more useless luxury products, a shrinking middle class employed in unnecessary bullshit jobs that allow them to aspire to do the same. Soylent, prescription opiates and Netflix for the rest, who dwell in the immense planet of slums patrolled by drones and robot soldiers.

Ironically 'the end of capitalism' has become a tangible possibility because capitalism has won. The great struggle of capital is that of freeing itself from the people whom it feeds on. Automation of work through robots and computerized production processes has been driven not only by the quest for productivity, but also by the desire to get rid of unruly workers, ever since the introduction of the assembly line in the 1920s. The construction of ever more efficient surveillance mechanisms, from barcode scans in the 1980s to Facebook today, has created a system where consumer demand is more predictable than before and unruly desires less of a problem. But when people no longer create a nuisance for the process of capital accumulation, when capitalism has rendered itself independent from its workers and consumers, there is no longer much pressure to innovate.

Outcasts

Like the declining feudal system of the European Late Middle Ages, contemporary capitalism is creating a massive exodus. As the feudal system developed, the pressure of feudal lords increased. They required more resources to engage in costlier wars and, importantly, new forms of conspicuous consumption became necessary at the foremost royal courts. Some, mostly in England, even became capitalist, using their lands to graze sheep for the growing wool market, and effectively evicting whole villages. This created a great exodus from the countryside. People who were no longer able to make a living in their villages sought their luck in the cities. Throughout the Late Middle Ages these 'masterless men' fuelled the many peasant revolts and millenarian movements that proliferated. But not everyone fled because they had to. Some also went to the cities in search of a freer, more modern life, attracted by new ideas of equality and freedom. Today as well, we see a massive exodus from capitalism. The children of the Western working class face growing unemployment as do, increasingly, the downwardly mobile middle classes. In the South the combination of climate change, the privatization of land and the allure of global consumer culture, visible on billions of small screens across the world, has created a massive migration to the cities, where the number of migrants far surpasses the possibilities of employment in the official capitalist economy. Like in the desolate *banlieues* of the North, this has created giant slums and a sprawling informal economy, often guided by criminal interests. Again, some of these people leave because they have to. But many also leave because they do not see any prospects for a meaningful life in capitalist employment. This is most apparent among middle-class knowledge workers who soon realize that a corporate career will not give them the possibility to realize themselves and have an impact in the way that they were taught in college. But even the popular classes are fleeing the factories if they can, choosing riskier but more fulfilling pursuits, like small-scale entrepreneurship in the bazaar economy, over the rigours, humiliation and boredom of factory work.[26] The future promises a further intensification of this scenario as automation will replace more sections of white-collar work (as it did with blue-collar work in the 1990s), and the digital economy is threatening traditional brick-and-mortar business in sectors like retailing (that traditionally absorbed those laid off from the contracting industrial economy in the West). The advance of digital technologies is likely to further intensify the polarization between a declining core of well-paid jobs and a growing periphery of precarious employment that was set in motion by corporate outsourcing in the 1980s. In emerging economies, the situation has been different – so far. Now, however, automation and the vertical integration of supply chains has reduced the demand for industrial labour even here, and over-production of college graduates has begun to destabilize the obvious link between a college degree and a stable comfortable corporate career. Across the world, the industrial economy is simply employing fewer people in ways that are stable and desirable, while the global workforce is growing.[27]

At the same time as the old system has become less able to live up to its promises, its ability to make such promises in the first place has grown massively. The decline of industrial capitalism is paired with a massive increase in the reach and intensity of its commercial culture. Across the globe, the lifestyles that consumer culture promotes are visible on television screens present in even the poorest households, on ubiquitous advertising billboards, in the posh shopping centres that make up spectacular monuments to consumer modernity in the world's booming megacities and not least, on internet platforms like Facebook or Instagram whose users number in the billions. In this way material marginalization – being unable to afford the lifestyle promoted by industrial modernity – is combined with symbolic inclusion, people still aspiring to it or even feeling entitled to it. The life lived with an iPhone in hand looms like the unreachable mirage of a millennial capitalism motivating even the dispossessed to take risks and gamble with their lives, like investing the family savings in a precarious passage across the desert and the Mediterranean. Of course, the combination of pull and push factors is not entirely new. The serfs who fled to the cities in the European Middle Ages were also attracted by the prospect of relative freedom and autonomy; the puritan craftsmen and petty traders who sailed off to New England in the seventeenth century were attracted by the prospect of a social order based on equality and meritocracy. But today the global reach and scope of the promise that a different life is possible is arguably unrivalled in history.

At the same time as capitalism appears to be retreating from both production and social demands, the expansion of its metabolism has generated new kinds of commons. The networking of the world that has developed in the post-war years, and in particular with the growth of digital technologies, has meant that things – people, ideas, plants and species – are lifted out of their original local and particular context and circulated throughout the system in new ways. Skills, ideas or productive methods that used to be local or particular thus become generic and commonly available. These new commons act as an essential support for digital capitalism, enabling the growth of social media companies, of platforms like Amazon or Uber, and making it possible to outsource material and, increasingly, immaterial production to a flexible and precarious, yet at the same time skilled and competent workforce, equipped with similar skills across the world.

One way of seeing this process is that capital has expanded its metabolic processes to reach deep into the intimacy of the lifeworld, subsuming life itself and transforming it into capital that can potentially be exploited in all of its moments – nothing is safe anymore; love, friendship, sex, hunger, everything can be transformed into an asset that contributes to the capitalist accumulation process. However, this complete transformation of the common lifeworld into capital also means that capital itself, as a productive asset at least, has become common in new and radical ways. We will discuss the nature of these new commons further on. The point for now is that just as they act as a resource of capital accumulation, they are also deployed in new kinds of productive activities that move outside of, or even in opposition to, the crumbling edifice of digital capitalism.

The contemporary crisis of capitalism thus seems to be putting in motion a highly particular kind of dialectic. The re-feudalization of capital and its retreat from productive activities creates a growing exodus of unemployed or precarious people who, at the same time, seek out life projects that are independent from the ever less attractive rigours of salaried work. At the same time, the extension of capitalist metabolic processes to involve the very basic processes that sustain human life has generated new commons in the form of (mostly) digitally mediated skills, competences and connectivity. The outcasts from global capitalism use these new commons to realize alternative productive networks along with alternative life forms. The process does not quite resemble the dialectic of capitalist resistance that we are used to from industrial modernity. There is no new 'movement' intent on taking over the forces of production. Instead, an important aspect of the contemporary forces of production has already been socialized to the extent that it has come to coincide with the relations of production, or which is the same thing, ordinary social relations *tout court*. At this point the creation of an alternative takes the form of a re-appropriation rather than a revolution.

3

The Industrious Economy

The onset of industrial modernity changed everything. It sent all the curves spiking. From population, via energy use, to atmospheric concentrations of carbon dioxide, everything accelerated as Europe and the 'West' cut itself off from the rest of the world in the nineteenth century. This Great Transformation, as Karl Polanyi called it, also created a rift in the consciousness of the people who experienced it: a sense of loss for a past that seemed, in retrospect, more pristine, authentic and true, as well as great enthusiasm for a future that appeared to have already been laid out and found its direction. Indeed, industrial modernity came with a plan and direction. It promoted grand-scale transformation, often at the cost to both 'people and planet' (to use contemporary parlance). This kind of modernity depended on the new industrial relations of production. Industrial capitalism favoured large-scale investments, the overall transformation of national or even global economies, the standardization of production around grand transformative innovations like the automobile or the electricity grid, along with a substantial disregard, or at least innocence, about their environmental effects, on nature and on pre-existing cultures and ways of life.[1]

However, industrial modernity is not the only kind of modernity that is possible. Today, as industrial society is crumbling around us, we are seeing the seeds of a new kind of *industrious* modernity. Or perhaps this is, in part, a return of an ancient condition. Industrious relations of production can be characterized as small scale and labour intensive. The industrious economy remains rooted in traditional, or at least local, social relations. It draws on the common skills and competences that these convey. It is oriented to lived needs and use values that are expressed on fairly transparent and egalitarian markets. These are the relations of production that Adam Smith described in his famous example of the butcher and the baker who gave him his breakfast 'not from their benevolence [...] but through their regard to their own interest'. Such interest was, however, not yet paramount, but remained inscribed in a context where moral sentiments not only counted, but were fundamental, also to economic life. In industrious relations of production, the economy had not yet been lifted out of its social context and relegated to abstract 'expert systems'. It remained thoroughly embedded in the mundane concerns of everyday life.[2]

Industrious relations of production were typical of advanced pre-capitalist economies, in Late Medieval and Early Modern Europe, as well as in Ming and Qing China, in Medieval India and, even earlier, in the Islamic Empire. These were economic contexts marked by a prevalence of small-scale, labour-intensive production, by slow and piecemeal innovation rooted in local or artisanal traditions, by a mixture of markets and communitarian organizations like guilds and fraternities, and by a certain distance between the concerns of capital accumulation and the transactions of everyday economic life. True, there are many examples of the contrary such as the brutal 'primitive accumulation' that marked the commercialization of agriculture in England starting in the fourteenth century, or the colonial plantation economy that supplied most of the fuel for the European Great Divergence starting in the second half of the eighteenth century. But for the most part, capital moved at the aloof level of what Fernand Braudel called Grand Commerce, the world of finance, long-distance trade, colonization and similarly risky but potentially profitable ventures. Economic life, for most people, was closer to the *longue durée* of the everyday.[3]

Industriousness entails a mentality of making do and adapting to what is at hand. It is informal, entrepreneurial, street-level, *bricolage*. It does not require much capital and virtually everybody knows how to do it; it can be done on a fix. Industrial is the world of high tech, of path-breaking innovations: atomic fusion, cybernetics, genome mapping. Industrious, on the other hand, is the world of small-scale bricolage or *Jugaad*: of adapting new technology to new needs; finding a new market niche; making the internet a social medium through the invention of chat rooms and online forums; inventing a new app that combines long-established technologies like mobile payment; database management and social media data, or adapting cell phone technology to the needs of Chinese peasants. It is a world closer to the needs of everyday life, more preoccupied with use values than with cornering markets and investing in grand schemes. In technical terms, the industrious economy tends towards a natural, Smithian equilibrium, using available resources in new, more efficient ways, but without significantly expanding the 'Edgeworth box' of overall opportunity.[4]

To an expanding industrial modernity, such industrious relations of production seemed like an obstacle to progress. Messy bazaar economies, dirty street vendors, inefficient artisan workshops and the infamous labour-intensive wet-rice agriculture that, until the 1960s, appeared to condemn those practising it to eternal underdevelopment within the confines of a static 'Asiatic mode of production'.[5] Yet such 'traditional' industrious relations of production remained, often at the periphery of economic life, even in developed industrial economies. Digital technologies have brought this industrious middle layer back into the centre again. This is not principally a matter of a quantitative shift – Western job markets are still dominated by large-scale corporations; indeed, the share of people employed in large companies vis-à-vis small companies has increased in recent years. It is rather a matter of a qualitative shift; in certain sectors, in particular among knowledge workers, the industrious economic activity has become a new alternative. In this way, the industrious middle layer, far from being 'traditional' or 'immobile', is becoming central to innovation in the digital economy.[6]

Popular industriousness

In Shenzhen, China, the skyscrapers and shopping centres of the booming metropolis are covered with advertisements for Apple's new iPhone. A few blocks away, hidden a couple of storeys up in an electronics centre, there is another bustling market. Tightly packed crowds of young workers and students swarm around hundreds of small stands that repair and enhance your iPhone. They will change the screen, the battery or the chip set. They will modify or customize it, combining different cases with different components. They even claim to upgrade an iPhone 5 to an iPhone 6 or 7. They do it all with components – cases, screens, batteries and processors – that come from the very same factories that manufacture for Apple's supply chain. In the electronics market, you can personalize your iPhone, adapting it to your needs and tastes beyond the rigid design choices imposed by Apple, and you can prolong its life beyond its planned obsolescence.

Some of the people manning the stores actually used to make iPhones in Foxconn's nearby megafactory, and others worked in factories located in the supply chain for one of the many Original Equipment Manufacturers (OEMs) that in turn work for Apple, Samsung or some other major electronics brand. In short, they knew their phones, inside and out. Most of them are rather recent arrivals from the countryside, first-generation city dwellers. After all, Shenzhen itself has grown from a small fishing village in the early 1980s to a 17 million megacity today. They still have their roots in the 'village rationality' of rural China, a mentality marked by hard work and piecemeal adaptation to changing ecological and social circumstances – from flooding to arbitrary taxation – of finding a niche and making do. Once they lost their industrial jobs, or left them, it was not so hard to set up shop in the electronics bazaar. Like many people around the globe – the traders in Delhi's bazaars who have gone from selling used garments to peddling electronics, young victims of the Asian financial crisis in 1997 who went back to selling noodles on the street just like their grandparents did, albeit with a branded 'hipstery' feel to it – these young Chinese workers are adapting a traditional industrious mindset to the new digital economy.[7]

You can see the similar things in any global city if you look close enough. In the suburbs and the run-down inner-city neighbourhoods, like in Shenzhen's electronics market, you will find small shops and street vendors peddling cheap electronics or knock-off fashions made in China, along with family restaurants and services directed at the poor, mobile recharging and repair services and money transfers. While popular industriousness, the economy of what French anthropologist Alain Tarrius calls 'poor-to-poor', has always been there at the bottom layer of the industrial economy, it has grown in size and importance in the last decades. More people are either cast out from the lives they used to live in the countryside or in working-class neighbourhoods, or tempted to try their luck in cities that are unable to absorb all of them within an official labour market that is itself contracting. At the same time, digital technologies and the new common resources that they make available enable them to organize economic networks more easily and more efficiently than before, creating in effect a global bazaar economy connecting peddlers in Paris and New York to small Chinese factories in Shenzhen and Yiwu via Dubai or Istanbul.[8]

Particularly for young people in poorer contexts, carving out a market niche in small-scale retail, tourism or new growth sectors like mobile communications has become a way to avoid the perils of looming unemployment. Growth in the mobile telephony sector has been particularly spectacular. Small shops selling sim cards and subscription plans, offering to convert mobile currency credit (like the East African Pesa), or simply offering to recharge the cheap phones with short battery life that are most commonly used, proliferate in bazaars and street markets. Some offer more sophisticated services like decoding or unlocking locked phones, or offering to repair or replace screens or other broken parts. These businesses use specialized software, often downloaded for free off the internet, and rely on advice in global 'hacker' forums and chat rooms. Overall, a large, often informal economy has developed around mobile technology, mostly composed of small street kiosk businesses operating on the cheap.[9] Along with mobile technology there has been an increase in small retail operations selling counterfeited or 'pirated' goods. These are frequently goods with a high symbolic or 'immaterial content', like knock-off bags or fashions or cheap electronics. Often these are produced in small labour-intensive factories that have, in turn, emerged out of the global outsourcing of manufacturing. Their capacity to respond quickly and flexibly to market demand, along with the establishment of complex distribution chains composed of global 'suitcase entrepreneurs' who import or sometimes smuggle small shipments, has led to the creation of a global economy of 'memefacturing'. New trends and fashions from global internet culture are translated into material goods with astonishing speed, as in the case of the Chinese-made Obama Phone that enjoyed brief success in Kenya around the time of the 2007 US elections, or the more recent global hoverboard craze.[10]

The success of Shanzhai cell phones (and other electronic products) illustrates this well. Starting in the mid-2000s, Shenzhen became the centre of the world's pirate economy as petty traders arrive with suitcases from Lagos or Delhi to buy up cheap and cheerful Shanzhai (or 'pirate') cell phones to distribute on street markets throughout Africa, Asia and the Middle East. At its peak in 2008 the Shanzhai 'system' produced 200 million cell phones a year and was largely responsible for making mobile connectivity generally available, and not just something for the rich and privileged. (It was estimated that in 2008, 30 per cent of the world's cell phones were Shanzhai. Arguably, the people who tweeted on Tahrir Square in the 2011 mass protest mostly did so on $20 Shanzhai devices.[11]) The Shanzhai production system was organized around small design houses surrounded by networks of component manufacturers, who might also work for larger brands. The design houses were quick to design new phone models on the basis of what they understood to be new market niches and organize the production processes through informal networks, using Open Design practices. The operation was extremely rapid as a new design could go to market in as little as one month, as compared to one year in the case of giants like Samsung and Apple, and stay on the market as long as there was a niche to exploit. Then the manufacturing network dissolved and new projects were launched. The whole process was premised on extreme flexibility along with the ability to cultivate an advanced 'feel' for the market and what it wanted and could support.

Overall, the global counterfeit trend has increased massively in recent years, as a result of industrial over-capacity, improved networking and knowledge sharing even in informal supply chains, and a growing demand from less resourceful consumers who, nevertheless, are able to participate vicariously in the trends of global consumer culture. This suggests that the corporate economy is losing control over the bottom end of its supply chains. Having relocated production to small, labour-intensive factories in low-wage economies, the globalization of production has at the same time generated overcapacity and made common the trade secrets that used to guarantee corporate control over production. Now this commons-based productive capacity is re-appropriated by a popular industrious economy made up of relatively capital-poor actors who maintain deep roots in an ordinary everyday existence marked by needs and desires that they share with their customers. As the head of a Shanzhai design company claimed, Shanzhai entrepreneurs are people from simple backgrounds who keep asking themselves 'what will the normal people need next'.[12]

Such 'globalization from below' or 'pirate modernity' offers an industrious alternative to the official world of shopping centres and corporate brands. It has played a vital role in giving popular access to even advanced electronic goods like dvd players and gaming consoles, along with the brands and designer fashions that make up the material culture of global modernity. While the pirate modernity used to be a phenomenon of the 'South', of the bazaars of Delhi or the street markets of Lagos, it has increasingly poured into the cities of the North as well. Since the 1970s, immigrant entrepreneurs in Northern Europe have traditionally set up small-scale labour-intensive businesses like family restaurants or small retail or export/import operations, providing similar kinds of services first to their communities, and increas-ingly to poorer members of the 'aboriginal' former working and middle classes as well. In Northern Italy, working- and middle-class youth buy their cloths from the 'Chinese' sellers who peddle cheap and cheerful fast fashions in neighbourhood markets (made in China, or in small-scale Italian garment factories, sometimes themselves operated by Chinese entrepreneurs). They dine at the many counterfeit (or Shanzhai) sushi restaurants that have proliferated in inner cities, set up by young Chinese second- (or third-) generation migrants with relatively modest capital investments and providing an affordable dining experience with an exotic flair.[13]

Bourgeois industriousness

However, industriousness is no longer simply a strategy for the poor and marginalized.

In up and coming inner-city neighbourhoods, and in reclaimed industrial spaces in the suburbs, or in the many co-working spaces that now proliferate along the global nomad trail, from Chiang Mai via Bali to Lisbon, you instead find university-educated knowledge workers slaving away over their computers. They dress differently from their peers on the street, they have different world views and more ambitious plans to realize themselves and 'change the world'. They mostly produce immaterial things, business plans, design, events and communication campaigns or other kinds of projects (although knowledge-intensive, neo-artisan material production is making a comeback with the popularity of 3D printers and cheap and accessible numerically controlled machinery). Like the peddlers in the global bazaar economy, they are also outcasts, either because they are unable to find a corporate job despite their expensive education, or because they had one and got fed up with it. And they are similarly precarious and eke out a modest living, if they earn anything at all. Most importantly, their activities are capital poor and labour intensive. Digital technologies have made it possible to start companies, design websites or organize complex forms of collaboration spanning across the globe with much less capital than before. (Since 2000 the average costs of launching a start-up are said to have declined a hundred-fold, from $500,000 to $5,000.)[14] This is because digital technologies have themselves become more efficient, less costly or even free to use. They offer access to a vast repertoire of common goods – from free software to YouTube tutorials and design templates. At the same time, these industrious knowledge workers work much harder than their parents (or even their older siblings) did. In part this is because of the proliferation of digital technologies. Always-on smartphones along with the need to be constantly present on social media have meant that the boundaries between work and life have collapsed. In part it is because skills like business model planning or social media management have themselves become generic and common, and consequently, even knowledge workers are forced to work long hours to survive.

This entrepreneurial turn has been significant enough to leave its mark on aggregate statistics. In the US, the share of new entrepreneurs who have a college degree has increased by 30 per cent since the mid-1990s, bringing entrepreneurship among knowledge workers, who used to prefer stable employment to such ventures, up to the level of the population as a whole. Figures are similar in Europe, and current tendencies in rapidly growing countries like India and China point in a similar direction.[15]

The most visible aspect of such knowledge worker entrepreneurship has been the wave of start-ups that has sprung up in cities worldwide. *The Economist* famously referred to the proliferation of start-ups as a 'Cambrian Explosion' of business ideas. But in hindsight this appears to be largely a misnomer. Most start-ups are rather about incremental innovation, combining existing technologies and business concepts to carve out a new niche: an Uber for bread, a new kind of sharing platform, or a new application of data analytics. Similarly, the potentials of blockchain technology have been expanded to the limits of human imagination. (The list includes games for breeding potentially precious 'Cryptokitties' and blockchain apps for securing future mining rights on asteroids.) Even before blockchains, the app economy based on relatively simple and standardized programming languages had significantly widened the scope of start-ups. Apps can be used for social innovations that transform everyday problems or issues into business opportunities. Similarly, the popularity of social entrepreneurship has meant that areas that used to be the purview of politics or philanthropy have opened up to entrepreneurial intervention, leading to a proliferation of apps and platforms that, often unsuccessfully, aim at 'changing the world' in some way, mostly by following a standardized repertoire.[16]

This expansion of often similar entrepreneurial solutions applied to marginally different niches is a direct result of the commonly available technological and organizational tools that have proliferated as a result of the spread and intensification of digital culture. Commons-based peer-production (CBPP) has generated a host of free or openly available solutions. In the last decades CBPP has expanded in scope, moving from the provision of software and immaterial goods (like freely available online encyclopaedias or courses) to forays into design and material production, as with the fab-lab or Maker movement. The world of CBPP shares some of its culture and demographic with the start-ups. Indeed, many start-uppers are also active in peer production projects (this is a way to keep up with skills, and not least require a reputation that can be capitalized on in different ways). Conversely, many CBPP communities generate 'archipelagos' of start-ups around them or seek to organize small enterprises into a business commons, where revenues are distributed fairly and risks are shared. At the same time CBPP provides an important share of the new knowledge commons that in turn fuels the start-up economy. The availability of free software and open communities of practice in which to acquire and cultivate skills has contributed massively to radical decline in capital requirements. This has made the contemporary flourishing of start-ups possible.[17] Shared technological platforms like smartphones, social media, proprietary collaborative software like Google Docs along with the availability of a new repository of skills and knowledge in global digital culture is another important part. So is the industrial over-capacity that results from corporate outsourcing. For example, it is common for hardware start-ups to use Kickstarter or similar crowdfunding platforms for initial funding, and then rely on small-scale Chinese electronics factories for cheap and rapid prototyping. Shenzhen has seen the growth of a number of hardware incubators, mostly staffed by young entrepreneurs with engineering degrees. These incubators mediate contacts with local factories for prototyping and potentially manufacturing. At the same time, related 'social' technologies are creating local market niches to be exploited by start-ups and the app economy that they generate. For example, new global mobile connectivity is producing a new mass market that can be easily tapped into through the construction of relatively simple app-based services for transport, mobile payment, hotel booking or personal services. This is driving the emergence of a new generation of start-ups in countries like Nigeria or Cambodia that are new to digital markets.[18] As a result of these new global opportunities, start-ups and incubators are booming in the emerging economies of Asia and Africa, and phenomena like new forms of digital nomadism are in the process of creating a transnational group of knowledge workers that move from venture to venture in locations across the globe. Like the gap year, it seems, the start-up is becoming a common feature of the average knowledge worker's curriculum. It has become something of a replacement for politics as an outlet for the vital energies of a new generation, eager to change the world, but often without an overall plan for how to do it.[19]

A similar kind of incremental innovation results from knowledge worker entrepreneurship merging with traditional crafts. This has led to a proliferation of new kinds of high-end consumer goods and services. These neo-artisan enterprises are driving a quality revolution in the food economy. This is manifest in the proliferation of neo-traditional agricultural practices with accompanying farmers' markets; in the rediscovery of traditional forms of food preparation like craft butchers, bakers, brewers and distillers, and in the many food trucks that are proliferating in major cities across the world. It is manifest in the renewal of traditional craft trades like barbers and butchers, along with the fusion of artisan crafts and design, often with significant high-tech ingredients, like the use of 3D printing, laser cutting or open-design systems. The 'neo-artisans' who populate this 'hipster economy' are mostly university educated and they operate in a new urban service economy marked by a demand for quality and original goods and services. There is, however, significant contamination between this hipster economy and the informal economy that is itself booming, mainly in the cities of the South: Thai and Indonesian fashion designers make use of local textile sweatshops to produce creative spinoffs on mainstream trends and brands to be sold alongside genuine knock-offs in street stalls catering to workers and university students. Overall, the street fashion scenes of Bangkok and Seoul are driving an alternative fashion industry where their innovations are trickling down to reach popular markets for cheap low-quality garments. It is as if the rediscovery of craft production on the part of global knowledge workers is producing a quality and design revolution that is rapidly trickling down also to more popular market segments.[20]

The industrious economy, in its start-up, hipster and CBPP, and pirate versions, is marked by a common aesthetics of use value. Shanzhai phones might borrow brand images and other symbols from global consumer culture. These are part of a global symbolic common that is drawn on to confer a quality of modernity or 'brandedness' on products. However, this is done without caring much about the identity or significance of what the owners of these symbols might want them to convey (as in the case of blue jeans that combine the logos of Levis, Wrangler, Nike and Facebook). The intention here is to confer a use value on the product, and not to respect the identity of the brand. And the particular combinations of brand or commercial symbols might change very quickly, as consumer demand and preferences change. Indeed, the aesthetics of Shanzhai goods are determined in dense networks of face-to-face communication, where traders and consumers interact in bazaars and street markets and the results of such interaction is relayed onto highly flexible design operations. Rather than an attempt to control and structure markets, as in the industrial use of brands and consumer culture, aesthetics is a reflection of a continuous state of proximity to consumer demand, and the ability to respond rapidly to changing tastes and preferences.[21] The hipster economy shares a similar orientation to use value, only that here the source is understood to be the intrinsic complexities of goods themselves, rather than manifestations of actual demand. In order to be successful in providing craft beer or artisan coffee, it is crucial to be passionate about the metaphysical qualities of the product that one has dedicated oneself to, and to cultivate a community that shares such passion. The start-up and CBPP sectors are similar; here, too, 'passion' is a necessary condition for participation. One has to believe in one's product or service, in its ability to 'change the world'. And one is evaluated according to one's ability to provide use values that contribute to a particular product, be this simply to 'write beautiful code' as Gabriela Coleman found to be the strongest motivation of people participating in the Debian free Software project. We will come back to culture and motivations of the industrious economy below. Suffice it now to say that, contrary to the industrial economy, where profit is a principal motive, the industrious economy is marked by a combined orientation to market exchange and to the cultivation of the values that define excellence in a particular practice or product. It takes the form of continuous adaptation and tinkering, of market driven small-scale innovation, of what digital entrepreneurs call 'permanent beta' where feedback and response can be rapidly incorporated in a product that is conceived to be in constant evolution or flux.[22]

The Bangkokization of the world

Start-ups and food trucks are generally small and labour intensive. People work long hours and earn little money. Apart from a few success stories of nerds going from rags (or rather college hoodies) to riches, figures indicate that start-ups (including maker-oriented ventures and enterprises in the hipster economy) perform much worse than traditional small companies. Indeed, in his reportage on the 'Flat White Economy' of coffee shops, craft breweries and tech start-ups that has grown in London's East End since the financial crisis, Douglas McWilliams describes how this sector is premised on the massive availability of young, qualified and enthusiastic university graduates from all across the world. They are willing to work long hours for comparatively low wages while shouldering considerable entrepreneurial risks. Writing in 2015, he notes how 'Champagne sales are down a quarter since their peak in 2007' while the number of cups of coffee sold has increased by 50 per cent in the same period. This is not simply an indication of impoverishment. It also testifies to a lifestyle change. Champagne is consumed after work, at the nightclub or at the party. Coffee, on the other hand, is consumed at work, while coding away in the all-night coffee shop.[23] Studies of start-ups and hipster entrepreneurs in Asia show similar results. The multitude of small-scale fashion designers who populate the night markets of Bangkok or Jakarta or the 'creative neighbourhoods' of Chinese cities – and recently Instagram and platforms like Taobao as well – generally do not make enough money to sustain themselves, but live off of other resources, like second jobs or family resources. This pattern had been well established in Western 'creative cities' for a long time and fieldwork in the start-ups scenes of Delhi, Bangkok and Taipei indicate the same thing: most people who embark on these careers either have a corporate background to fall back on, or significant family resources to live off. This is also the case for the self-employed knowledge workers who represent the absolutely largest share of knowledge worker entrepreneurship. Indeed, from a strictly economic point of view, the incomes generated by start-ups and high-level 'hipster' service enterprises seem to indicate a convergence in productivity levels between knowledge work and traditional forms of low-skilled service work, like cleaning, driving or food preparation.

The skills upgrade that marks today's industriousness, the fact that intellectuals are embarking on a survival strategy that used to be genuinely popular, and, at the same time, that competences that used to be the purview of intellectuals are themselves becoming more diffused, leads to a convergence between intellectual and popular forms of industriousness. This is visible in the convergence of productivity levels between knowledge worker industrious enterprises, and industrious enterprise in the service economy.

Taking a 'helicopter view' of the phenomenon (to use management speak), the present state of the digital economy looks less like a succession of sleek high-tech start-ups and more like something of a Bangkokization of the world: When the Asian financial crisis hit in 1997, the Thai economy went into a ten-year recession. (Indeed, the crisis itself was triggered by the collapse of the Thai baht.) Skyscraper construction was abandoned, leaving cement skeletons over the Bangkok skyline, later to be squatted by homeless people and activists, and virtually a whole generation of college-educated knowledge workers were thrown out of their corporate careers. Along with them, a generation of rural migrants who had come to the city during the boom years of the 1990s lost their factory jobs. Together they triggered an industrious 'revolution' made up of a massive increase in street vendors, motorcycle taxis and other small-scale service enterprises. The inflow of college graduates into this industrious service economy produced a skills upgrade, giving rise to a series of branded street vending operations, small bars and designer coffee shops and a host of small fashion, music and design operations, driving the development of Bangkok into a creative hub in the subsequent decade. While separated by strongly engrained class differences, these popular and elite industrious entrepreneurs worked side by side, sharing the same urban spaces (like the night markets) and the same production networks (fashion designers would, for example, rely on over-capacity in small-scale garment sweatshops to create their collections). Most importantly, their earnings were roughly the same. Similarly, important cultural barriers and great differences in access to family backing and other kinds of resources separate the knowledge workers toiling away to build social enterprise start-ups that will change the world in Chiang Mai's or Bali's co-working spaces from the motorcycle taxi drivers who drive them back and forth to their backpacker hostels. From a strictly economic point of view, however, productivity levels in the two sectors are converging. Downwardly mobile middle-class knowledge workers are joining small-scale entrepreneurs from popular backgrounds in a global industrious economy that is labour intensive and capital poor and where, consequently, earnings (with some notable exceptions) remain low.[24] Together they rely on the new commons that digital capitalism has created through its metabolic expansion throughout the global lifeworld.

The industrious ethic

This digitally empowered industrious middle layer is also converging around a common economic ethic. The concept of an economic ethic goes back to Max Weber's classic writings on the origins of modern capitalism. To Weber, capitalism and modernity was brought about by the industriousness of the protestant puritans. They worked hard, not simply to make money, but because they found a sense of purpose in labouring for a future, as of yet unknown but pregnant with promise. Indeed, Weber suggested that more than anything else, the puritans were driven by a calling. They believed that dedicated hard work was a Christian duty, the right way to further God's work in the world.

Weber set their industriousness apart from two other ways of engaging with economic activity. The first is the traditional way, the comfortable way of merchants in some (perhaps imaginary) traditional society, before the great upheavals of modernity. Here the pace of economic life was slow, change was gradual and above all work was understood as a means to other ends, as a way to achieve a comfortable life. There was no use investing too much energy or passion in it once a sufficient standard of living had been arrived at. 'There was time for long daily visits to the social club and, occasionally, also early evening drinks and long talks with a circle of friends. A comfortable pace of life was the order of the day.' The second is what he defines as the spirit of modern capitalism, oriented towards endless accumulation as a goal in its own right. Indeed, Weber suggests that the strength of this unachievable goal, which has come to dominate the economic mentality of modern life, rests on the fact that it has been institutionalized. In modern life, endless accumulation, greater efficiency and continuous improvement has become an institutionalized imperative. It is a goal that one has to keep aspiring to, whether one believes in it or not. It is no longer a passion or even a choice, as it was for the puritans. Instead, endless accumulation has become part of an iron cage, to use Weber's terms. 'The puritan wanted to be a person with a vocational calling; we must be.' This way of acting and thinking is no longer a matter of belief or dedication, rather 'it is bound to the technical and economic conditions of mechanized, machine-based production'.[25]

For the protestants breaking with traditional life *before capitalism*, hard work was instead undertaken with dedication; it was informed by a subjective passion or at least a sense of meaning and purpose, in some sense a calling, if not necessarily a religious one. A similar attitude prevails among actors in the contemporary industrious economy.

'For us, entrepreneurship is not about money, it is about passion, commitment and activism', as the keynote at a recent co-worker unconference told me. In a modern *industrial* economy, hard work might similarly be driven by dedication and subjective passion, but it does not have to be; in fact, more often it seems not to be. Instead, hard work is a necessity; it had been institutionalized in a series of command and control systems, ranging from the brutal to the subtle, and it is the only way forward, or even to stay afloat. Often such industrial work is perceived as alienating and soulless, a theme that runs through virtually all of modern critical social theory.

There is another side to these very same observations, however. Industriousness is a form of economic action that emerges when the iron cage is broken, when there are no longer any sufficient institutional moorings that supply meaningful goals and a sense of purpose. When one has to create such a sense of meaning and purpose oneself. Industrial work, work in the iron cage of modernity might have been boring and soulless but at least it was safe. Not simply in an economic sense, although steady careers, health insurance and pension plans certainly helped, but also in an existential one. You might not have liked your job as a postman or a mid-level bureaucrat, but at least it gave you a sense of purpose, a reason to get up in the morning, a respectable identity and a reasonably predictable view of the future. When these things are no longer given, one has to make them up oneself. For Weber's puritans, people whose livelihood and sense of identity were no longer anchored in a traditional order that was now crumbling under the pressure of an advancing modernity, working hard became a way of convincing themselves that their life had a meaning and, that, importantly, the future was, in some way, predictable. Indeed, the puritans of sixteenth-century England were in part 'masterless men' gathered in cities where the puritan sects offered protection from the vagaries of an insecure life. This applied in the material sense of offering food and housing as an alternative to vagrancy and petty crime. It also applied in the spiritual sense of offering a sense of purpose and something to believe in. As Michael Waltzer suggested a long time ago, the condition of 'masterlessness', of having no

given place in a changing world, was a fundamental prereq-
uisite for their success. The puritan industrious ethic allowed
people to find 'a new master in themselves', in the form of
a rigid self-control shaping a new personality. 'Conversion,
Sainthood, repression, collective discipline were the answer
to the unsettled conditions of society.' For the puritans,
industrious work also served to anchor an existential project.
That existential project was oriented towards a future,
which, however, remained abstract and unknown.[26]

Today, as the industrial order is crumbling around us,
dedicated hard work also becomes a way of convincing
ourselves that we are doing something meaningful, that what
we are doing is important (that we have an impact) and that
consequently we have a status (a reputation). Perhaps most
importantly of all, when the future is uncertain, hard work
makes it seem, if not predicable, then at least made up of a
succession of projects that each comes with calculable risks.
The transformation of fundamental uncertainty into calculable and actionable risks, is no longer performed by the
institutions of Weber's old iron cage, but must be achieved
by working passionately for something we believe in, be this
changing the world, the sublime aesthetics of craft ale or
simply ourselves. Indeed, perhaps today such industriousness
has become the most important existential response to the
precarity that comes with systemic collapse.

Indeed, like for Weber, today's industriousness is closely
linked to the notion of entrepreneurship. It is as an entrepreneur that you can change the world. This is not simply
a matter of economic change. Rather entrepreneurship had
become something of an existential project. Schumpeter
wrote that the role of the entrepreneur is that of breaking
with tradition and 'act[ing] with confidence beyond the range
of familiar beacons'. Perhaps more importantly though, the
role of entrepreneurship today is that of creating a cultural
framework that allows such confidence to emerge. More
than Schumpeter, Frank Knight comes to mind. He suggested
the entrepreneur is a person who is able to confront radical
uncertainty and transform it into something that can be
acted upon, into a set of calculable and actionable risks.
In the end, the most important component of industrious
entrepreneurship is to invent a narrative of the future that

domesticates it and renders it actionable and, in a certain sense, predictable, if only in an imaginary way. Indeed, a recent post in the Chiang Mai Global Nomad Facebook group complained about the ubiquitous presence of 'actor-preneurs': people who printed business cards, curated their social media platforms, constantly talked about their start-up ventures but in the end did not actually produce anything of value. Rather than 'real' entrepreneurs, such *actorpreneurs* were engaged in performing entrepreneurship as an existential project, as a way of coping and surviving.[27]

At the same time, the scope of entrepreneurship has expanded. Lifestyles, political objectives or social causes can now lead to the creation of a business. A number of universally available business templates, like the influential Business Model Canvas, help with this, as do countless self-help books, seminars and YouTube tutorials. Influenced by design thinking (which itself has begun considering social processes and not simply material things as objects of design), these offer a 'shared language for describing, visualizing, accessing and changing business models'. Here a business is not necessarily understood as a money-making enterprise. Rather a business is a generally efficient way of intervening in the world and designing a solution to a problem or a response to a need. This has extended thus the scope of business itself from a purely economic practice, to one infused with a plurality of existential concerns. As one influential guidebook addressing the new 'microbusiness revolution' explains: business 'is a way of earning a good living while crafting a life of independence and purpose'.

At least in the official rhetoric; in the guidebooks, Post-it workshops and TED talks that animate contemporary industrious entrepreneurship, the order of priorities has been reversed. Creating a business is, *first and foremost*, about finding meaning and purpose, and only then, as a consequence, possibly about making money as well. As one famous motivational speaker put it in his TED talk:

> What's your purpose? What your cause? What's your belief? Why does your organization exist? Why do you get out of bed in the morning and why should anyone care? By 'why', I don't mean to make a profit. That is the result, it is always a result.

It would seem that entrepreneurship is ever more under-stood as a way of escaping the iron cage of industrial modernity, to exit from its economic rationality, to 'fire your boss, do what you love and work better to live more' to once again quote the guidebook.[28]

It is as if the economic rationality of industrial modernity, painstakingly achieved through a long and intense process of social engineering, is losing its grip. For many knowledge workers at least, work and enterprise are not primarily about economic gain. Angela McRobbie and her colleagues stress this about the Berlin fashion entrepreneurs whom they interviewed. These entrepreneurs are mostly young, university-educated people who work long hours and make but minimal earnings. 'Almost none of the respondents spoke directly about a business plan as such, nor did they make much use of the term "brand". One or two even mentioned that to begin with there was no commercial aspiration whatsoever.' Fashion, quite simply, was not a thing that one did for money. For the Milan-based designers, interviewed by the same team: 'the key thing was to be working, to have status and self-respect and to emerge out of the cloud of unemployment and of being turned down for jobs. In addition, it was the sociality of working against the isolation of staying at home.' To work and no longer be unemployed was primarily understood as an existential benefit; to be able to experience oneself as doing something meaningful, and to have that experience confirmed by others. It was not primarily about making more money. Work, for these fashion designers, was first and foremost an existential rather than an economic practice.[29]

To some extent, this might be because there is not that much to gain from such work, anymore. In interviews with workers in the Milan fashion industry some ten years ago, people claimed to love their job and state very high levels of job satisfaction on the quantitative scales that were used. This was despite the fact that their earnings were insufficient to maintain them in the expensive city where they worked. (Median income was €800 and 59 per cent declared that they depended economically on their families. The median age of the sample was 38 so these were not just student trainees.) Still they loved the fact that they were 'creative'.

(Even though very little of what they did when they worked could be understood as creative in any meaningful sense. It was mostly about arranging communication campaigns and events in a context of office discipline that often bordered on the despotic.) But they could experience themselves as creatives, as participating, materially day by day in the creative world of fashion, and that was the point.

It might be justified to think that this highly singular motivation is particular to fashion, a field that has traditionally attracted young people ready to make substantial sacrifices in order to get a foot in the door. But research suggests that it is more of a general phenomenon. (After all, fashion, art and, more generally, 'creativity', has developed into a model for contemporary knowledge work overall.) Ten years later, interviews showed similar results with self-employed knowledge workers in co-working spaces; with start-uppers; with 'neo-rural' university-educated farmers returning to the land to engage in high-quality, ecologically conscious farming; with food trucks; and with people who participate in numerous peer-to-peer projects ranging from software to hardware and 'making'. Earnings were low across the board, too low to support even a minimum standard of living for the overwhelming majority (again family resources helped). However, job satisfaction was high. The general feeling was that the future is uncertain, but at least I am doing something about it. As McRobbie and her colleagues also remarked in their study: work and entrepreneurship function to solve existential issues on a personal and social level: 'one is, once again, a somebody', and this, not the often elusive economic gains, is the main point.[30]

The economic situation is not necessarily this bleak for all knowledge worker entrepreneurs. Some do make money, and many dream of the unlikely prospect of making a lot through a spectacular exit. Recently the token economy that has developed around blockchain start-ups offers possibilities for more advantageous forms of remuneration. But the existential rewards come first. Indeed, it is usually invoked as a motivation for leaving behind an economically rewarding but existentially unsatisfying corporate career in favour of something much riskier and less profitable, but, in the end, more meaningful. Richard Ocejo's ethnography of new craft workers in New York showcases a world almost entirely populated by people who have exited the corporate world at some stage, to embark on a low-paid, relatively insecure, but existentially satisfying career. As he writes of the middle-class 'kids' taking up (what used to be) working-class jobs like bartending or butchering, albeit with a highly refined 'hipster' aura to them: 'These workers get cool jobs, but not because they're cool or want to be cool. For them, getting one of these jobs is the result of a search for meaning in work, to get recognized (by both consumers and people in their occupational community) for what they do, and for an occupation to anchor their lives and provide them with purpose.'[31]

That 'millenials' prefer existential self-realization over economic rewards has become something of a truism, and as a truism it has come under scrutiny by empirical research.[32] However, there is a long tradition of research that backs up a similar trend, at least among relatively privileged and resourceful knowledge workers, without necessarily generalizing these to a single generation. Already in the early 1980s – long before the millennials – management scholars began to point at the growing problem of 'managerial flight' or 'managerial cynicism'. Mid-career professionals, in particular after five to ten years on the job, tended to become less enthusiastic about the 'rat race', more difficult to motivate and above all more cynical about attempts to make them embrace corporate culture. Indeed, the long tradition of 'values-based management', corporate branding, motivational seminars or 'wellness' that has since accumulated, can be understood as an attempt to come to terms with such new, 'post-material' preferences.[33] At about the same time, the dream of leaving the corporate world behind, to move to the country or embark on a pursuit that is more wholesome, 'real' or satisfying began to enter popular culture. Since then, the mid-level manager who resigns to move to the countryside to painstakingly produce his own business cards out of recycled textiles has become a cliché. The dot.com boom of the 1990s rendered mainstream the notion of knowledge work as also, or even primarily, existentially rewarding. Rather than the grey Orwellian reality of organization men, new digital work was about self-expression and a revolutionary redrawing of boundaries, individualism against the masses, as Apple's famous 1984 Macintosh commercial stated. In the dot.com offices of the 1990s, and in their successive incarnations in the creative industries and the Web 2.0 start-ups of the following decade, work was organized to be intense, yet fun, meaningful and self-realizing, at least in theory. Indeed, as media historian Fred Turner has suggested, the new digital work that emerged at the turn of the millennium represented a wholesale introduction of countercultural values, like self-realization, personal meaning and social purpose into the rhetoric of mainstream managerial discourse. Like Steve Jobs or Mark Zuckerberg, you might get rich, but that was not the main goal. Like them, you got rich, primarily as a way to change the world, to impose your own highly personal vision on it, to use it as material for your own self-realization.

Disruption

As Regis Debray has suggested, the idea that business is a matter of 'changing the world' by imposing your own personal project on it testifies to the continuity between today's industrious ethic and the ethic of the early protestant entrepreneurs that Weber discussed. It is, however, a continuity with a number of twists to it. In Europe, the radicalism of the protestant sects and their obligation to do God's work in the world through business was tempered by worldly powers. Calvin eventually gave in to Luther, and for most people the religious vocation became a compromise between the radical impetus of the calling and the inertia of an established social order. In the US, on the other hand, the radicalism of the new protestant sects found fewer obstacles in the form of traditional authority, as Alexis de Toqueville observed. Instead, the American protestant social vision evolved into a sort of spiritualization of the market. The world appeared to be made up of two poles: the divinely inspired vision of the entrepreneur on the one hand, and the market as the ultimate arbiter of her virtue on the other. Gone was the social world with its complex obstacles and power balances that had preoccupied European political philosophy from Machiavelli to Gramsci and Lenin. If you had an idea, go for it; if God liked it, it would work out.[34]

This is of course a gross over-simplification of the history of American Protestantism. However, that tradition did generate an important figure of thought that informs its contemporary ideological off-springs, religious as in the case of globally successful prosperity gospels, and lay, as in the case of the multitude of self-help manuals of the Oprah Winfrey variety. There the *Secret* (the title of perhaps the most successful manifestation of this genre) is that your ideas can change the world. If you believe in something strongly enough, desire it strongly enough, it will come true. Translated into Silicon Valley speak, this becomes the doctrine of 'disruption' – the idea that a singularly powerful idea, aided by technological means, can change the ways in which the world works. This can be a matter of changing the ways markets work, or of solving some pressing issue, like world poverty, through a stroke of technological genius that bypasses the complexity of politics, policy and social organization. (Soylent along with universal basic income!) In the end the market is the judge; if the entrepreneurial power of the disruptive individual or team is strong enough, rewards in the form of venture capital and market growth will come forth.[35] And like the protestant preacher, the successful entrepreneur never stops. She continues to disrupt the world, spending her wealth in doing so. Once he has disrupted the way in which people relate and socialize, Zuckerberg wants to go on to disrupt the ways in which civil society and politics works. His wealth is but a means to keep doing so; the reward lies in the spiritual fulfilment of realizing his vision and himself.

In its singular disregard for the complexities of the social world, the doctrine of disruption continues the tradition of the US Second Awakening that accompanied the industrial revolution. Here 'the ideal type of the believer on the make [like those born from Horatio Alger's pen], was required to blot out enormous swaths of economic and social causation as they actually existed to invest the heroic market attuned features of the self with a correspondingly great power'.[36] The ability to actually 'blot out huge swaths of economic and social causation', not only theoretically, in one's wishful thinking, but also actually, in one's business plan, has in part been made possible by that comprehensive project of social and cultural engineering that many now refer to as 'neoliberalism'. As a project, neoliberalism has managed to almost eradicate the social from discourses (if not the reality) of society, replacing it with the market, populated by entrepreneurial individuals (and, as Margaret Thatcher added, their families). In this way, individual success or failure falls back on the individual herself, on her entrepreneurial spirit, on her power to endure competition. Conversely, powerful individuals and ideas will succeed as market forces, independently of the resistance offered by residual social forces. The concentration of the power of change to the individual also brings in another continuity with the tradition from early Protestantism: if the individual is an enterprise, then maximizing the utility of her time is a top priority. And failure to spend one's time well (in acquiring skills, for example) is understood as an important cause of failure. This Franklinite doctrine of time (and human capital) as value, plays out in innumerable coaching and self-help programmes (like the many lists of *Habits of Successful People* that spam the social web), as well as in more disciplinary programmes aimed at the not sufficiently entrepreneurial poor (like programmes that force the unemployed to spend their time learning new 'skills').

The fostering of such a neoliberal entrepreneurial self has a history that goes back to at least the 1980s, and it has since come to infuse almost all aspects of what Michel Foucault called 'governmentality', from schools via self-help gurus and unemployment offices to prisons and career coaches. However, it would hardly have become as successful in dominating our thinking had it not found support in the material conditions of our present existence. Most social scientists agree that the intensification and objectivities of time is one of the most important consequences of the mass diffusion of digital technologies. The combination of new forms of work that blur the distinction between labour and leisure, and always-on digital connectivity has generated an overall objectification of time. All time can potentially be used productively, for business as well as, importantly, for pleasure. When you are not working, you should be experiencing things! This supports an ethos where, as Hartmut Rosa puts it in his theory of what he calls 'social acceleration', 'the maximal enjoyment of worldly opportunities and the optimal actualization of one's own abilities has become the paradigm of a successful life'.[37] However, even more than the technological objectification of time, it is the lack of an overall goal or purpose to it that seems to work as the main motivation for the contemporary industrious ethic. Time is not only objectified, but the future that it leads to is also uncertain, and that is what really makes people dedicate themselves to their work, in the here and now.

Like for Weber's puritans, the most important satisfaction that can be gained from an enterprise that changes the world is existential. Even though Weber showed how membership of 'protestant sects' had a number of immediate practical benefits, like access to what we would call 'social capital', the spiritual dimension was central. Hard work served to prove to oneself, to experience that one was among the chosen few. For today's industrious entrepreneurs, rewards are similarly practical and immanent. They rest with the distinct practice that one is involved in. To be part of something and to be able to experience that every day. To work with the 3D printers and the laser cutters that embody the future, and to be a 'Maker'. To go to pitches and the networking events and to be a start-upper about to disrupt things. To be a social entrepreneur engaged in changing the world.

This immanent, experiential aspect is not exclusive to creatives. Alex Rosenblat's study of Uber drivers suggests that at least the ones who do it as a second job tend to be motivated mostly by the social experience. Studies of Airbnb hosts show the same thing: even if the monetary component is important, most stress the social, experiential aspect as their main motivation for what they do – to get to know people, to feel that one is part of the 'sharing economy' (whatever that is).[38] In some cases, the experience is not even discursively articulated but simply gamified. One Deliveroo rider in Milan that we interviewed explained that he understood his job as a continuous competition with the app, and kept going in order to beat parameters that it imposed on him. It was a combination of computer games and fitness, only that you got paid! Uber has experimented with similar strategies of gamification to motivate their drivers to take on additional rides and work longer hours. And if we want to count in the constant 'work' that we all perform on social media platforms – our daily iSlavery to use Jack Qiu's term – then countless studies show how the main motivation for picking up the smartphone throughout the day is a carefully engineered hope of a small satisfaction in the form of a like or a comment. Gamified enjoyment, at the heart of what Alfie Bown calls Candy Crush capitalism, could be understood as sort of degree zero of the contemporary industrious ethic. Indeed, research on the industrious economy tends to bring forth a striking contrast between the projections of a disruptive future that venture capitalists and other investors require, on the one hand, and the fundamental orientation to the present and its experiences that mark the worldview of most workers and small-scale entrepreneurs.[39]

Communities

We are beginning to see the two poles of the contemporary industrious ethic. On the one hand, at its heights the Steve Jobs and Mark Zuckerbergs of this world project their self-realization onto the world through a series of disruptive innovations, backed by massive amounts of capital, aiming to change the world according to their vision, and never mind the messy realities of politics or social organization. At the bottom end, the precarious workers, self-employed or not, who seek a series of experiences, be these simply small gamified satisfactions that can postpone for a moment an ever-looming anxiety. Most members of today's industrious sector find themselves somewhere in the middle. For them, lofty ideals of disruption soon crash with the actual complexities of the world, and experiences are for the most not entirely empty affects but actually about something.

They are, for the most part, anchored in communities of practice like peer-to-peer communities, start-up scenes, co-working spaces, communities of craft beer connoisseurs. Indeed, the term 'community' is constantly present in the discourse of contemporary industrious modernity (even when such community seems to be absent in anything but the ideal). In part, this is because communities are vital to the collaborative work that marks contemporary industriousness. They are mechanisms that enable the sharing of knowledge and skills and contacts; places 'where ideas have sex' to quote the device of a co-working space in Milan. Communities are repositories of the knowledge commons that makes advanced economic activity possible at little cost. True, you can learn how to code or build a brand from YouTube, but it is only in a community of practice that you get to know the real application of such abstract knowledge. Communities are also vital for existential support. In our study, industrious communities, peer-to-peer communities and co-working communities (often painstakingly supported by a community manager) work as a constant source of collective enthusiasm. Mailing lists distribute news and titbits that enhance the meaning and significance of the practice that the community engages in. In this way communities build the idea of the specific activity at the heart of the community (Making, Free Software, neo-traditional foods) as pregnant with a significance that goes far beyond the economic. A similar enhancement of the importance of the community and the practice that it is dedicated to also inspires the many social events that most such communities organize: seminars, networking events or attempts at involving the outside world through neighbourhood events. It is through the community that a practice, otherwise perhaps difficult to appreciate, becomes enriched and acquires meaning and value.

Communities are spaces of encouragement and support. News of member success or positive events, however modest, meets with collective cheer and encouragement. As one speaker at a recent co-working conference defined the approach in the community that he had helped set up,

> At [our co-working space] we really encourage any tiny win that you could just think of, like sending your first invoice. Because it's so easy to get bogged down in negativity thinking 'I am never going to make this, I am never going to make any money.' So by celebrating all the little steps along the way it gives the people the idea that it's gonna be hard but they can actually get there, by celebrating the little things everybody just feels great, it's a nice mood lifter for the whole space.

We celebrate everything. We publicize everything. We go 'we have this amazing team and they just did this, how fucking awesome is that?' and it's such a great space when everybody is celebrating everything: fuck ups are awesome too.

Max Weber's puritans accumulated capital through 'compulsive saving'; today's industrious modernity is oriented towards the accumulation of social capital through compulsive celebration. These communities provide a source of recognition and reputation that enhances the existential meaning of a pursuit. Such a sense of recognition can support members through difficult economic times, and compensate for a lack of general social recognition for the sometimes arcane practices that they are dedicated to (video art, Arduino, bio hacking). This precious affirmative function of communities also explains their often uniform nature. Co-working spaces celebrate diversity and underline the importance of true personality. Yet, the tolerance for real difference is often limited. Strict, often informal rules for speech, behaviour and self-presentation exist and violating them leads to sanctions. Carolina Bandinelli documents the dire consequences of bringing supermarket, non-organic chicken to the Tuesday brown bag lunch at a London-based social entrepreneur space. Or, as one community manager whom we interviewed put it: 'Only people who are OK with our model come here.'[40]

Communities enrich practices and provide them with meaning. This way, the short-term economic precarity that comes with engaging in industrious activities can be balanced by a long-term sense of existential stability. I might not be earning much today, but at least I am doing something that people whom I respect recognize as meaningful.

The infusion of work and entrepreneurship with affectively laden, meaningful experiences is in many ways a consequence of the neoliberal destruction of politics and the social. Thus, work has been posited as an existential pursuit of personal self-realization. At the same time, there are few other available venues for expressing concerns that go beyond the economic. A number of issues used to be addressed through political action, formally addressed to the state rather than the market and least officially devoid of an economic dimension (although the New Social Movements of the 1960s and 1970s did originate a lot of entrepreneurial activity). Now these forms of collective mobilizations are largely gone and entrepreneurship is left as what appears to be the most efficient and 'modern' way of addressing a number of issues that go beyond the strictly economical. Even explicitly political social movements tend to take a decisively entrepreneurial form, realizing social enterprises, or as in the case of Italy's movement of occupied theatres and art spaces, or oppositional market mechanisms organized though alternative currencies. Even when these movements stake an explicitly political stance, their methods remain highly entrepreneurial, addressing specific local problems in ways that combine market action and community activism.[41] In addition, the new availability of common resources and versatile technological platforms means that the number of issues that can be transformed into an entrepreneurial project with relative ease has expanded. As politics in the old sense becomes more difficult and cumbersome to engage in, enterprise becomes easier and appears to be the natural choice. This also points beyond the neoliberal 'death of the social'. For some people, industrious entrepreneurship is becoming a new kind of politics, a way of furthering a plurality of values and agendas that are concerned with building alternatives to the established order. In the contemporary industrious ethic, neoliberalism is perhaps finding its dialectical negation. When business and enterprise has come to invade all areas of existence, the political as well as the personal, then enterprise is also, inevitably, politicized in new ways.

This is not simply a matter of adding values and passion to fundamentally economic pursuits. Rather politics in some sense is fundamental to contemporary entrepreneurship. This is obvious in its more politicized varieties like social entrepreneurship, the archipelago of business practices that are forming around CBPP or the range of new blockchain-based start-ups that sometimes have very radical business ideas. Here the explicit purpose of business is to build a new social world, to reconstruct the social around technologically empowered ideas that have the ability to fundamentally change the ways in which markets, production, consumption, transport or energy systems operate. However, such a constructive, political element is intrinsic to the very idea of disruption itself. A successful start-up, even if it is simply in it for the money, needs to be able to argue that it is constructing a new reality, that it is changing the world in some way, because that is what sets it apart from others.

At the heart this has to do with the productive conditions of a commons-based economy. When capital requirements and barriers to entry are low, when the skills and competences needed are commonly available and easily apprehended, the only alternative to cut-throat competition is diversification. In a condition of fundamental insecurity, such diversification happens at the intangible level. You have to construct an intangible quality around your product, project or persona in order to enrich it and give it a value that sets it apart from everyone else. The way to do that is through a practice that is very close to what the moderns considered the political: to mobilize and build an affectively charged community of people and practices around your proposal: to engage in what Max Weber called political entrepreneurship.[42]

Such political entrepreneurship happens at the personal level; you have to show that you have something immaterial and intangible that others do not have, a virtuosity that sets you apart from others. It happens at the level of commodities, which need to be differentiated from functionally and aesthetically similar goods. They require a process of enrichment whereby their singular qualities can be apprehended. It happens at the level of investment and access to capital. It is by showing that one's team possesses a singular entrepreneurial capacity, and not simply a good idea (which, in start-up parlance is in any case 'cheap') that one can convince an investor to release the funding. In all these areas it is the performance of a singular immaterial quality, of virtuosity, which is the key to success.

The performance of such singularity happens through processes of enrichment that involve communities of practices. Above all, it involves the construction of a standard against which a practice or a product can be evaluated. Peer communities can thus set the standards by which your ability to cooperate and to further the common cause are set, and then implement the mechanisms by which it is given explicit or implicit value. It is through their collective judgement that your human and social capital is valued. The value of organically farmed pre-industrial grains or craft distilled gin is set by communities of practice, involving consumers, producers as well as other actors, who create the possibility of an experience that warrants substantial price differences. This experience is seldom simply one of taste, but one that is also pregnant with the promise of a different ethics. Pre-industrial grains not only taste better, but they also come pregnant with the promise of a different way of organizing agricultural production and consumption, or even the revival of the values of a more authentic and humane 'peasant civilization' that have been lost in the process of modernization.[43] In this 'ethical economy', value and the performance of virtue, in the sense of an all-round virtuosity in furthering the values to which a particular community is dedicated, come to coincide. In many ways, the logic is similar to what Weber described in the case of the protestant sects in the US. Membership of a sect and conduct that was virtuous according to its standards were crucial in order to acquire the kind of reputation and societal standing that made possible successful business practice within the community. Like the protestant sects, today's industrious communities are pregnant with a politics, yet to be articulated in its specific details and manifesto. This politics is at the same time anchored in economic practice. As in the case of the protestants, this is an open-ended and constructive politics. It is not about defending any established ideals or manifestos (at least not yet). It is about constructing a new social order organized around a number of inherently distinct and largely disconnected ethical projects.

As an ideal type, the industrious ethic can be summarized as an existentially motivated, labour-intensive entrepreneurial mindset driven by an empty calling. A calling rooted not in the certainties of futures past, but in the dual immanence of existentially significant experiences in the here and now on the one hand, and market performance on the other. Like the protestant ethic, it applies fully only to a small minority, but it informs, at least in part, a growing mass of entrepreneurial subjects aiming to create a meaningful future for themselves and their peers beyond the failing promise of industrial modernity. This industrious mass is composed of the ideologically integrated, yet increasingly materially marginalized of this world.

True, far from everyone works for a calling. The labour intensity of the capitalist economy has grown in the last decades and a lot of this is due to masses of low-paid hard work that is not self-motivated. Slavery is rampant throughout the modern economy, as is the habitual violence practised by the likes of Foxconn factory guards and the *caporiali* managing gangs of African migrants working the tomato fields of Southern Italy. Yet even for the most disempowered, it is the lure of entrepreneurship that looms as the most feasible exit strategy. The possibility to opt out of the boredom and humiliation of factory work, to open up one's own shop, to be one's own boss is what motivates the small-scale factory entrepreneurs that fuel the Shanzhai or pirate economy; the stalls of illegal iPhone hacking or jailbreaking that you find in the backstreets of Shenzhen's electronics market; the peddlers of cheap electronic goods 'free port Dubai' along Europe's sultan route. Indeed, for what such figures are worth, the 2016 Global Entrepreneurship survey reports that about two-thirds of entrepreneurs in poorer 'factor-driven' economies stated that they had chosen this path out of choice rather than necessity. In richer 'innovation-driven economies', the figure was only slightly higher, 79 per cent. As two Chinese sociologists describe the motivations of the micro-entrepreneurs in Yiwu who set up shop producing cheap, uncomplicated consumer goods like cigarette lighters or plastic knick-knacks for the export market, most come from peasant backgrounds, and most have moved into the city and embarked on entrepreneurship as a way of getting ahead in the world. But an overwhelming majority frame this 'getting ahead' in terms of lifestyle and existential change, rather than simply the accumulation of money: 'we can see a big difference from the parents' generation in that young entrepreneurs from poor families regard personal development as more important than earning a living. They move from rural to urban areas not just to earn more, but to seek opportunities to change their lifestyle.' Here the entrepreneurial choice is economically informed, it might even be an economic necessity, but it is generally framed in existential terms, as the realization of a personal project, as the ability to make a change in the world, if only the small world of one's own life. As Claudio Sopranzetti writes of the motorcycle drivers of Bangkok, often former factory workers who have chosen a riskier, more precarious entrepreneurial path:

> Itsaraphap (freedom, independence), many of the drivers like to repeat, is what keeps them in this hectic stressful and health-threatening occupation. The drivers acknowledge job insecurity and the risks of road accidents, and they often resort to the protection of amulets and magic tattoos. Nonetheless they insist – as do many other workers in the urban service economy – that the job's itsaraphap makes up for the precarity of their labor. As Yai, the vice president of the association of Motorcycle Taxis of Thailand (ATM) told me, staring into my eyes, 'motorcycle drivers die young, but live free.

Of course, not all of these existential projects can be said to be creative, in the sense of combining action and work in the sense discussed above. Some can simply be attributed to the raw attraction of a global consumer lifestyle that embodies globally shared, if abstract ideals of modernity. But even this consumerist dream comes with a project of existential autonomy. As Sanjay Srivastava writes about the inhabitants of Delhi's working-class neighbourhoods, 'they do not entirely succumb to the lifestyle models of consumer modernity, but they fashion them to their own lives and their requirements, if anything, the market is perceived as the source of empowerment and control over one's identity and destiny'. Even at its most mechanized and organized level, the Candy Crush capitalism that organizes contemporary iSlavery, the continuous interaction with smartphones and similar gadgets constitutes an industriousness that is fuelled by the possibility of autonomy and personal impact, if only in the form of an ever illusive 'Instafame'.[44]

For the knowledge workers of the world, including those in rapidly growing contexts like India and China, an embrace of the industrious ethic with its call to 'change the world' can be understood as an attempt to revalue a cultural capital that is in the process of losing its economic convertibility. In lay terms, my university education no longer lands me a job but it allows me to embark on a practice that I can understand as not only existentially meaningful but also as a form of virtuous action, or even something of political significance. Indeed, a host of more or less cynical sociologies of bobos, the 'aspirational class' or 'hipsters' have explained this dynamic in terms of an ongoing competition for positional goods.[45] And while these explanations might make sense from a sociological point of view, they do not undo the potential of this new industrious ethic. Even if entrepreneurial creativity is simply a way of reproducing cultural capital, the fact that cultural capital is reproduced this way entails new potential. The protestants that Weber wrote about, or at least their spiritual ancestors, were also people who found that their skills and talents no longer had value in the old system. Dissident intellectuals, heretic priests, then as now, were the 'thought leaders' who embraced the new outlook to the fullest, joined later on, in different contexts by the masses of labourers and disenfranchised peasants, to form the multitudes that together created modern market society and its critics. Today we are seeing the beginning of a coming together of popular and intellectual exponents of contemporary industriousness, as the world is connected and networked in new ways. For them, hard work informed by an industrious ethic becomes a way of creating new life in the ruins.

4

Industrious Capitalism

According to Braudel, the industrious economy is not a 'true capitalism'. Rather it is capital poor and labour intensive. Actors tend to engage in market competition, rather than, as large capitalist corporations seek to do, dominate markets. As we have seen, actors are not simply motivated by the instrumental logic of capital accumulation, but embed such economic rationality in wider value horizons. This does not mean that the industrious economy is outside of or untouched by the power of capitalist corporations. Some of it is, but on the whole the (re)emergence of an industrious middle layer has also coincided with a restructuring of the capitalist economy, so that capital accumulation now tends to depend increasingly on the ability to control and 'subsume' a multitude of industrious actors that are, at least formally, external to capitalist corporations. In other words, the emergence of a non-capitalist industrious middle has made capitalism more industrious as well.

Indeed, the industrious middle layer is in part an effect of the last decades of capitalist restructuring. (The lower layer economy that Braudel observed in Prato in Italy in the 1970s was to a large extent a consequence of the contemporary transformation of the Italian industrial system, leading to a growth of a multitude of similar 'industrial districts' that engaged in small-scale 'flexible specialization'.[1]) In the

1980s and 1990s, multinational companies embarked on a wave of outsourcing, relegating material production to smaller firms located in the emerging economies of central America, East Asia and China. In these global supply chains, a growing share of material production was shifted from an industrial mode, employing large amounts of capital and relatively well-paid workers, to an industrious mode, relying on intensive labour by low-paid workers with relatively little capital at their disposal. This tended to create a dual labour market. On the one hand, core employees in corporate headquarters were employed in functions related to the control of flows of goods, money and information. They were well paid, in part because of their relatively rare skills and cultural or social capital necessary for the production of increasingly valuable intangible assets. On the other hand, peripheral employees employed in manufacturing were located along global supply chains, deploying commonly available skills and little capital, and earning significantly less. This dual labour market further expanded urban markets for labour-intensive low-paid services as a new middle class of corporate workers demanded new and more advanced forms of personal services, sometimes supplied by actors in the informal economy.[2] Soon enough, the process of outsourcing proceeded to involve more generic forms of 'immaterial' labour as well, starting in the 1990s with outsourcing of back-office operations and call centres to countries like India and the Philippines. The growing market for services, both corporate services and customer-oriented services, which marked those decades, further enhanced the scope of small-scale labour-intensive operations working outside of corporate organizations. Consequently, the 2000s saw a significant outsourcing of more advanced corporate services, leading to a growth in so-called 'creative indus-tries' – communication, design, marketing and branding and event organization. (Significant, albeit mostly unsuccessful, efforts were also made to locate such creative industries in rural areas as well as in former industrial cities in decline.)

Capitalist outsourcing has thus contributed to generating new demand for small, labour-intensive enterprises, often one-person operations. (Although, until recently, similar labour-intensive forms of production have been employed by gigantic original equipment manufacturers (OEMs) like Foxconn, employing millions of workers in a single factory. However, Foxconn has plans to replace 10,000 workers with robots, in 2019.[3])

With crucial assistance from digital technologies, industrial capitalism has recreated the industrious economy it had sought to absorb and eradicate only a few decades ago. So far this has not meant that power is transferred to smaller actors, or that we are now witnessing a new industrial divide in its 'second', 'third' or 'fourth' version, where the future belongs to small innovative companies operating in 'democratic' markets with high degrees of trust and transparency. Instead, most small companies or actors are subordinated to large corporate actors who themselves have become significantly more powerful as a result of the process of outsourcing itself. This is particularly the case for the many self-employed who are now populating the labour markets of advanced economies.

However, the process of outsourcing, together with the rise of 'immaterial' production in the form of a service and brand economy, has also contributed significantly to the creation of new global commons.

The new commons

That capitalism has created the new commons might sound a bit unorthodox. The received wisdom in the tradition that, starting with Elinor Ostrom's work, has taken a new interest in the commons is that capitalism and the commons are inherent opposites. This perspective does fit the more recent historical experience. That guilds and commons stood in the way of an emerging industrialization and were eventually swept away by it, to the extent that 'most historical commons – at least in the Northwest of the European continent – had been largely eliminated by the end of the 19th century', is a well-known fact.[4] It is generally understood that the defeat of the commons, in the form that they had assumed during the European Middle Ages, was a precondition for the development of modern, industrial capitalism. This Great Transformation, to use Karl Polanyi's term, did not only entail the material enclosure of the rural commons and the legal dismantling of the urban guilds. The triumph of industrial production also rested on the defeat of a popularly rooted moral economy where market exchange was to be based on artisan labour deploying common skills, and rooted in a common morality. As Bonneuil and Fressoz describe what they understand to be a decisive moment in this conquest – so decisive in fact that they see it as a key factor behind our entry into the 'Anthropocene' (or 'Capitalocene') – the defeat of the 'machine breaking movement' of the late eighteenth century:

> The machine breaking movement was made up of urban artisans (typographers, textile workers) and rural labourers (peasants who spun, wove and knotted by hand, seasonal cereal threshers, etc.). They expressed their refusal to see themselves dispossessed of their skills, their livelihood and a way of life that combined agriculture with manufacture. They rejected poor quality industrial products and championed the idea of a fair price for their labour against the machines that were the cause of imbalance and inequality.[5]

To put it briefly, Karl Polanyi's Great Transformation was a process in which the commons became capital. Things ceased to function as assets in relation to production processes that were rooted in communitarian life forms and oriented towards the singular values that they embodied. Instead, the very same things – land, human bodies, culturally embedded skills and social relations – began to function as assets in relation to a unified process of capital accumulation that expanded to embrace the whole world market. As the rural commons were enclosed, they became capital to be exploited in new kinds of commercial agriculture. As the *commoners* left the land and entered into factories, their bodies were transformed into variable capital, embodiments of a new social force, generic and abstract labour. In their free time, their needs and desires were mobilized by an expanding culture industry and shaped into a similarly abstract 'audience labour', the source of a new and more predictable consumer demand. This process of capitalist appropriation of the commons still goes on, particularly in the Global South, where land grabbing along with military force, masked under slogans like the 'War on Drugs', is repeating the process of primitive accumulation of the early modern European countryside. At the same time, however, capitalist development has created new kinds of commons.

The idea that capitalism, and particularly digital capitalism, generates new kinds of commons that it cannot fully control or valorize is the cornerstone of many analyses of the digital economy. Most famously perhaps, Antonio Negri, Michael Hardt, Massimo De Angelis and other exponents of the Italian 'school' of autonomist Marxism have made this a key tenet in their analysis of contemporary capitalism. To them, contemporary informational or 'cognitive' capitalism builds mainly on the commons, in the form of everyday linguistic and affective relations as its main productive force. In processes of 'subsumption of life', these lived commons are mobilized into immaterial labour that produce the cognitive or immaterial assets like innovation, flexibility and brand.[6] Advanced capitalist accumulation builds on forms of social cooperation that are embedded in ordinary life processes and, therefore, not fully controlled by the wage relation. Intangible assets like brands or the capacity for flexibility or innovation are examples of this. They represent the ability to mobilize the utilization of common resources like digitally enhanced forms of communication, as we tweet or Instagram about brands.

This argument builds on the famous passage from Marx's *Grundrisse* retrospectively entitled 'The Fragment on Machines'. There Marx develops his analysis into seemingly contradictory conclusions. To simplify the argument: the more complex productive cooperation becomes – and the virtue of the factory system is precisely that of making new, more complex productive cooperation possible – the more it depends on skills and competences that evolve within the factory environment. How to operate a machine, how to relate to fellow workers and bosses, along with mastery of informal tricks of the trade are necessary to function productively. Such tacit knowledge, to use a term that has since become popular with management consultants, are things that one only apprehends by entering the factory and becoming part of its productive 'community', the worker acquiring it 'by virtue of his presence as a social body'.[7] This genuinely social knowledge that enables productive cooperation is subsequently embodied in machinery, which in turn mediates cooperation in new ways and thus generates new kinds of knowledge. The important thing is that the common knowledge, or General Intellect, thus generated is embedded in social relations that unfold beyond the direct control of capital and the wage relation; 'it is, in a word, the development of the social individual which [now] appears as the great foundation-stone of production and wealth'.[8]

> The development of fixed capital indicates to what degree general social knowledge has become a *direct force of production*, and to what degree, hence, the conditions of the process of social life itself have come under the control of the general intellect and been transformed in accordance with it. To what degree the powers of social production have been produced, not only in the form of knowledge, but also as immediate organs of social practice, of the real life process.[9]

To Marx the development of the factory system thus also entails a process of remediation of cooperation, whereby new social relations, new forms of 'commoning' are created within the factory system and these in turn come to generate and embody new kinds of commonly available knowledge, or General Intellect. At a certain point, this general intellect becomes the most important force of production – surpassing the 'theft of labour time' and here it is as if we go directly to 'post capitalism', not with a bang but with a whimper, as it were.

> The *theft of alien labour time, on which the present wealth is based*, appears a miserable foundation in the face of this new one, created by large-scale industry itself. As soon as labour in the direct form has ceased to be the great well-spring of wealth, labour time ceases and must cease to be its measure, and hence exchange value [must cease to be the measure] of use value. [...] With that, production based on exchange value breaks down, and the direct, material production process is stripped of the form of penury and antithesis. The free development of individualities and hence not the reduction of the necessary labour time so as to posit surplus labour, but rather

the general reduction of the necessary labour of society to a minimum, which then corresponds to the artistic, scientific etc. development of the individuals in the time set free, and with the means created, for all of them. Capital itself is the moving contradiction [!][10]

This stumbling into communism, through a process put in motion by the 'moving contradiction' of capital itself, whereby the new commons that it generates somehow become its negation, is the cornerstone of the political analysis of Italian autonomist Marxists, as well as of more popular and influential analyses that this tradition has inspired.[11] Something of the sort does indeed happen as this 'communism of capital' – to use Negri's term – is institutionalized in the corporation (indeed the term 'socialism of capital' was used by late nineteenth-century observers in relation to the rise of corporations).[12] Replacing exchange value and the market with bureaucratic control of the 'visible hand', the corporation becomes organized around the protection and cultivation of its proprietary intellectual capital. As becomes gradually more evident for economists and management scholars during the twenty-first century, starting with the path-breaking work of Fritz Machlup, the nurture of the corporate knowledge commons through managerial tactics that support continuous innovation, creativity or even collaborative communities, along with their legal protection through intellectual property law becomes the secret to success in the capitalist game in what became known as the 'knowledge economy'.[13]

Overall, contemporary digital capitalism is marked by the twin tendencies towards the outsourcing of production, often in the form of global value chains, and the financialization of value (already Marx saw the establishment of 'surplus value commons' and the shift to financial rent as consequences of the networking of capitalist production). The development of digital information and communications technologies (ICTs), starting with corporate intranets in the 1970s, can be understood as, in part, driven by the need to integrate a large number of actors, inside as well as outside of corporate organizations within extended forms of commoning, where knowledge and skills are shared. This happens implicitly as digitized instruction for how to create a specific component (like a touchscreen for an iPhone) are sent to a subcontractor. It also happens explicitly, as subcontractors are often contractually obliged to contribute to innovation processes.[14]

However, the digitalization of the capitalist commons introduces a particular dialectic. ICTs and technologies like CAD/CAM make possible the outsourcing of production to third parties. This also means that the technical solutions, skills and competences necessary to make a decently working washing machine become *common* in new and radically extended ways. The result, as management scholars Paul Adler and Charles Heckscher put it: 'the "mysteries" of effective commodity production have become common knowledge; they are now merely tickets for entry rather than keys to winning in competition.'[15] To use management speak, production, even advanced commodity production, has become 'commoditised'. It has become a common skill that millions of factories around the world, and maybe billions of workers, are able to engage in. It is possible that the coming new wave of automation, along with new digital infrastructures (what is known as 'the fourth industrial revolution' or 'Industry 4.0') will strengthen this tendency. (Many now speak of 'on tap' manufacturing: the possibility to make even technically advanced things as an instantly available resource at low cost.) As a consequence of the skills and solutions involved in manufacturing becoming common and generic, most commercial products have become similar to an unprecedented degree. Apple and Samsung are basically the same phone, they use the same technical solutions, and sometimes even the same factories. In fact, that is why they keep suing each other.[16]

In a similar way, the globalization of culture following on the deregulation of the media market in the 1980s and its subsequent networking via the internet has entailed a similar process. Nationally or locally specific traditions or lifestyles have been transformed into elements of a new global commons of planetary dimensions. With social media the details of the everyday life of billions of people have been transformed into a gigantic data commons, albeit almost completely controlled by a handful of corporations. Capitalist success builds on mining and appropriating these commons.

Branding is about combining specific forms of (in itself commonly available) productive knowledge with specific cultural features (in themselves commonly known) and using the (proprietary) data commons to insert the resulting hybrid into the daily life of the right people at the right moment. Logistics, of goods, of knowledge, of aesthetics and affect has become the key to success. Consequently, knowledge and managerial work has become a matter of creating singular combinations of such flows: it has become a matter of exercising 'creativity' or 'excellence' in ways that cannot be prescribed by a job description. At any rate, this has been the key suggestion of management thought, at least since the publication of Tom Peters and Robert Waterman's *In Search of Excellence*, in 1982.[17]

Start-ups and platforms

The last decades of capitalist restructuring have both contributed to and responded to the emergence of a new commons-based industrious economy. The response has been marked by a combination of outsourcing and financializaton, where gains are made not principally from productive activities but from the rent than can be extracted from controlling flows of finance and information. These twin logics mark the most important institutional responses that digital capitalism has developed to confront the new industriousness: the platform economy and the start-up system. They both share an important side-effect: the standardization of innovation and of business models.

The start-up system originated in Silicon Valley in the 1970s as new ventures producing silicon-based microprocessor 'chips' for the booming computer market required new forms of capital ready to take great risks for similarly great returns. It evolved with the dot.com boom of the 1990s to become the principal way of financing ventures into the, then, uncharted terrain of the online economy. In the last decade the number of start-ups, as well as of the basic institutions supporting them, like incubators (or accelerators) and venture capital funds, has skyrocketed globally. Incubators and accelerators have been promoted by public actors like universities, states and city governments as ways to promote innovation, to counter youth unemployment and to boost local economies. Like 'creativity' a decade ago, the entrepreneurial attitude fostered by start-up incubators has come to be seen as a way to give young people in particular an adequate mindset to deal with the insecurities of a precarious labour market, and to address and solve a number of social problems, from unemployment to petty crime.[18]

Incubators and accelerators are principally oriented towards the production of opportunities for venture capital investment. Venture capital is marked by a readiness to take high risks and to operate over a long time horizon. Significantly, venture capital is a branch of private equity. Shares in start-ups are not traded on public stock markets, but directly change hands between private investors. Indeed 'going public', through an IPO (or initial public offering) is (or used to be) the end stage of the start-up process, the stage in which the stock options are cashed in, the investment pays off, and the lucky start-uppers join the ranks of the Zuckerbergs of this world. This means that, prior to the IPO, which in any case tends to be postponed further into the future, start-ups have no obligation to reveal their performance figures and do not need to conform to standardized forms of periodic reporting.[19] This results in great insecurity. Further insecurity comes from innovative or 'disruptive' ventures aiming to construct new markets or deploy novel technologies in new, previously uncharted ways. The principal ways in which the venture capital system produces objects for investment is through the transformation of such insecurity into calculable estimates of risk that can be priced on the market.

The transformation of insecurity into risk happens in part through an estimation of the actual growth potential of a business idea. But this is not the most important way. A more important way is through the creation of an entrepreneurial personality. The future performance of a start-up is by definition uncertain, and the number of potential start-up ideas are abundant, particularly in a time of industrious mass intellectuality. This means that the investment risk that a start-up poses cannot be derived (or at least, cannot be only derived) from what the start-up team wants to do. Instead, the calculation of risk is based mainly on *how they will do it*.

In other words, one of the principal assets that investors look at are the entrepreneurial qualities of the start-up team. This means that incubators and accelerators principally exercise an educative function. Once a start-up team enters into one of these institutions, a lot of time is invested in teaching them to think, act and identify with a standardized notion of the entrepreneurial personality, including techniques for presentations, pitches and other forms of public speaking. To put it crudely, incubators and accelerators are principally about teaching presumptive start-uppers to think of themselves as a particular kind of (start-up) entrepreneur and to ensure that their thoughts, actions and demeanour can fit the standardized templates used by investors to calculate the riskiness of a venture. Start-uppers learn how to conceptualize their venture as a business plan using the correct template, how to speak and present in the correct way and how to think about themselves, their activities and their future in the correct, entrepreneurial way. Their entrepreneurial personality is subsequently tested in a multitude of pitches, presentations and events that sometimes borrow from popular television formats like *The Apprentice*. This way they learn how to perform the virtuosity that is necessary to enrich their idea so that it can become an investment-grade start-up.[20]

This purely performative aspect of the start-up career has grown more important as the number of start-ups and incubators has increased. It is relatively easy to get a small grant, seed money that allows a team to enter into an incubator and start working on the process. However, the sheer number of early-stage start-ups makes it difficult to reach the level where serious investment is attainable. In London's start-up scene, one needs about £10 million to acquire the visibility necessary to catch the attention of the large investors that have the resources to enable a start-up to enter the mainstream market and 'scale'.[21] This means that the first years of a start-up's career consists in the team learning to perfect their role as start-uppers so that they can jump through a number of increasingly narrow hoops, in order to arrive at the level where they can actually start working on their business idea. This process entails reducing the diversity of individual ideas and personalities into a common format where actions and intentions become calculable. Obviously, this also entails a standardization of conceptions of what constitutes innovation and entrepreneurship. Start-uppers end up thinking in roughly the same way about their business and about what constitutes a viable venture.

A second source of standardization comes from the portfolio thinking that guides venture capital investors. In a risky environment, a good strategy is to invest in a large number of similar ventures, hoping that one or two of them will make it. This means that outside of the relatively limited sector of start-ups that aim at commercializing genuinely new technologies (such as research spinoffs), most start-ups that are financed in a given period tend to propose fairly similar combinations of existing technologies. In the 1990s it was websites, in the 2000s it was social media platforms, recently it has been e-commerce apps and, importantly, 'sharing' platforms; now, increasingly, it is blockchain applications. If you wanted to acquire investment for your enterprise, you would have to make sure that it conformed to the business model currently in vogue. In 2010, whatever it was that you wanted to do, you had better do it with an app; today you better do it with a blockchain! These basic features of the venture start-up imply that, rather than stimulating innovation and disruption, it tends to result in a global standardization of innovation. As its actors and ideas, including ideas of what sort of ventures are attractive, spread globally, entrepreneurship around the world tends to be driven to conform to the same limited range of visions and business models.

In addition, the high rates of return on investment required as a reward for the large risks undertaken mean that there is an urgent need for a handful of successful ventures to pay off for all the others who did not make it. Consequently, the only commercially viable start-ups are those who have the potential to become global monopolies. This tendency is reinforced by the abundance of capital available, which tends to be concentrated to the actors that have already shown above-average growth potential, if only in terms of the potential to attract capital. In other words, as the only thing that will eventually pay off is a Facebook-style monopoly over a particular market, and because the only ones that are able to realize such a monopoly are the ones that have already received the greatest investments, new investments tend to go to start-ups that already have attracted large investments in the past. This self-reinforcing tendency leads to a quest for 'unicorns' (or 'pluricorns') who are able to attract investment in the range of billions of dollars, on the promise of them eventually being able to realize a worldwide monopoly over a particular sector of human activity. Some have been successful in doing this: Amazon, the most significant start-up to survive the dot.com era of the 1990s, has managed to effectively monopolize online retailing and is making a modest, if stable profit from that. Facebook, has, for now, managed to fence in a substantial part of the online advertising market and is realizing modest earnings from that.

Platforms

The closely networked, self-referential world of venture capital investors, the standardization of innovation that results from its culture and institutions, the abundance of capital-seeking investment objects and the high returns needed to compensate for all the failures, have all combined to promote the platform model of digital business as a 'winning' recipe. Platforms like Uber, Airbnb, Foodora, and before them Facebook and Amazon, build on the creation of proprietary markets. They use the potential of digital mediation to lower transaction costs in a particular sector. Their revenue models are based on owning the market, and on taxing the transactions that occur in it. Often their competitiveness rests on the ability of their algorithm to match supply and demand in new and more efficient ways. (The low earnings that Uber drivers make from an individual ride, for example, are partially compensated by the ability of the Uber algorithm to significantly reduce the down time when they are not driving.[22]) This tends to expand the market for particular services, or, sometimes, open up new ones. For example, Airbnb has vastly expanded the market for home rentals; delivery platforms like Foodora or Uber Eats have improved conditions for small-scale restaurants. The latter have also introduced a new category of actors, 'ghost restaurants' that simply consist in private kitchens with an attached website, working exclusively for the platform delivery market.[23] Sometimes these platforms have expanded business opportunities for small-scale operators. In Asia, Line has facilitated market access for a number of small-scale businesses, from restaurants to laundry services. Instagram and Facebook have enabled new small-scale artisans or vintage traders to find customers more easily. Sometimes platforms threaten to replace sections of the traditional industrious service economy. Laundry services, for example, are being 'appified' in Singapore and Thailand. Sometimes these pre-existing small-scale actors fight back. In many cities taxi drivers have been in conflict with Uber (or the Singapore-based competitor, Grab). Sometimes, like in Bangkok or Milan, the taxi drivers have won.[24]

In competing with the traditional industrious operators, the main selling points of platforms are ease of access and the standardization and sanitization of these services that they provide. Bangkok motor taxi drivers who drove for the Uber platform, for example, tended to invest in cleanliness and branding of their operations. In India, Uber and Grab have made a significant contribution to urban mobility, in particular for women, as these services (despite isolated events that testify to the contrary) are perceived to be safer than traditional taxis or pedicabs. Indeed, in contexts like India or China, the app economy caters to a new digitally networked middle-class market, where it provides services that are perceived, rightly or wrongly, to be safer, cleaner and cooler than pre-existing alternatives.

Platforms are symptomatic of the logic of contemporary re-feudalizing capitalism also in the sense that their business ideas build on retreating from the actual production of the products or services that they market. Platforms are based on the ownership of an algorithm and an interface that structures a market. The production of services is performed by platform users who, formally, operate as free contractors. These contractors supply most of the capital necessary to provide the service. Often this capital is already available to them. Airbnb began as a way to rent out free rooms. Even though the platform has attracted a number of entrepreneurs that invest in properties or make them up particularly for Airbnb, the platform remains a significant venue for people to commercialize assets, like second homes, that might otherwise not be used. Uber drivers provide their own car, petrol and insurance. Indeed, the platform started as a way for limo drivers to find work in their dead time. Recently the company has created a financing scheme whereby drivers can purchase new cars. But they remain independent entrepreneurs (if now in debt to the mother company, a strategy also used in corporate supply chains for a long time). Foodora or Deliveroo depend on assets like a bike and a smartphone that users provide themselves. Contractors are also formally free to manage their own time and make their own work decisions. In practice, however, this formal freedom contrasts with algorithmic management systems that nudge or sanction behaviour that is not optimal from the point of view of the platform. This means that platform workers often end up in conditions that are similar to that of managed workers, without the benefits that come with an employment contract.[25]

Significantly, platforms are able to compete with traditional providers, like hotels or taxi companies, not simply because of the efficiency of their algorithms, but also because they enable contractors to operate at marginal cost. If you already have a house, or a bike or a car, you can commercialize it at a price that need not cover the cost of capital needed to purchase it in the first place (at least in the short run). This principle means that the platform economy has significantly pushed down costs in a series of sectors and that, consequently, it is very difficult to make a living working for a platform alone.

Platforms and the venture capital system represent two important institutional frameworks that have evolved as part of an attempt on the part of the industrial economy to respond to the new industriousness. The platform model of algorithmically structured markets originates in the corporate platforms that developed in the 1980s to organize a new kind of decentralized, networked and increasingly self-organizing knowledge work. Instead of detailed individual job descriptions, these platforms used performance targets, various valuation metrics along with more abstract corporate values or corporate culture to nudge and guide self-organized labour processes in the right direction. The results were often an intensification of the labour process as excellent results, rather than merely fulfilling the requirements of the job description, became a condition for career advancement, or even continued employment. (Similarly Uber drivers have to invest substantial 'affective work' in achieving a sustained service rating of more than 4.5 out of 5, lest they be suspended from the platform.) In the past decades similar software architectures were used to structure globalized corporate supply chains, composed of hundreds or even thousands of independent actors, along with the complex logistics networks that they put in motion. The venture capital system began as a way to stimulate investments in uncertain technologies (like silicon-based microprocessors in the 1970s) to develop into a format for the corporate outsourcing of innovation and, increasingly, human capital development. Start-up ecologies flourish around the presence of big corporate actors like Google, Facebook, Apple, Amazon or IBM. These finance incubators and give out seed money, acting as a sort of latter-day patrons who promote a multitude of experiments with new uses of the technologies that they own or sell. Sometimes they supply Free or Open Source tools for such experimentation (Apple's IOS and Google's Android smartphone operating system is Open Source and is freely used by developers). This can constitute an important revenue stream in itself – Apple made $11 billion from its app store in 2016.[26] The most interesting innovations that come out of the start-up ecologies that they finance are bought up to be incorporated into the services of the mother company (like Instagram) or, simply to be closed down. In this way, a multitude of skilled, motivated and creative actors can be put to work in a kind of socialized R&D lab, at reduced costs. Significantly, venture capital and the platforms operate according to the same rent-based logic of value extraction that has constituted the most important capitalist response to the socialization of production and innovation. Consequently, the companies that result from this are compelled to seek world dominance. Facebook has been 'eating the web' for a long time, building an alternative position to Google through the development of its social graph and its expansion to more than 100 million sites with the Facebook 'like button', and has achieved a virtual monopoly on social media with its purchase of

Instagram and WhatsApp. Google and Amazon have created a world-wide infrastructure for search and e-commerce logistics, respectively. Uber and Airbnb is aiming at leading the market for their services worldwide. The hope here is that world dominance will enable substantial revenue flow resulting from the ability to extract a small tax from a large quantity of transactions.[27]

How good a response is this to contemporary industriousness? Platforms do open up new markets and expand existing ones. For a number of otherwise unemployed or underemployed actors, platforms have created a new source of earnings. Uber has been a popular choice for young men from the Paris suburbs, otherwise marginalized from the official labour market on account of their social and ethnic origins.[28] Freelancer platforms like Upwork have become an important part of creative workers' professional existence. Underemployed workers in the United States, often college graduates, use generalist platforms like TaskRabbit as a parallel source of income. However, earnings from platforms are generally too low for them to constitute the sole source of income for the people who work for them. Platform labour alone results in subsistence earnings, precarious working conditions and little or no security or benefits. Platform capitalism is unable to reproduce the labour power that it depends on. This makes it logical that several high-level exponents from the Silicon Valley establishments, for whom platforms are an important institution, have joined labour activists and social movements in proposing some form of universal income, if nothing else to cover the costs of social reproduction that platforms themselves are not able to cover.

The start-up system does not create a diversity of innovative enterprises that are able to sustain themselves on the market by catering to real needs and wants. Rather, it creates a series of essentially similar businesses that experiment with some combination of existing technologies without taking too much interest in what existing needs are. Its orientation towards rapid financial growth rather than market sustainability results in a large number of failures and a very small number of very large unicorns who effectively managed to disrupt or monopolize things. However, even those who make it are far from impressive from an economic point of view.[29]

Facebook and Google essentially share the online advertising market between them. But they realize fairly modest earnings from this. According to the latest available yearly results at the time of writing, Facebook realized earnings of $16 billion in 2017. However, relative to its market capitalization of half a trillion dollars ($536 billion as of 3 January 2018), this makes for a price to earnings ratio (a standard measure of company performance) of 33.5, or about twice the average for the Standard & Poor's 500 Index (S&P index). Google's performance is better, but both actors are nervous about the future of the online attention economy that they profit from. The oversupply of online advertising space along with mounting privacy concerns have decreased advertising revenues and made potential consumers more wary about and less attentive to ads. Amazon has lost money continuously until recently and only as the company has expanded to become the Walmart of e-commerce are earnings turning positive (from $274 million in 2013, to $3 billion in 2017). However, relative to investments, they remain modest (at 255, Amazon.com's price to earnings ratio is even higher than Facebook's). From the perspective of old-school, 'pre-disruption', Fordist economics, Facebook would need to double its earnings, and Amazon.com grow ten-fold in order to reach even average profitability.[30]

Companies in the 'sharing economy' are not faring much better. Airbnb is making a decent profit from its dominance over the home rental market, but half of it comes from an internal hedge fund that the company operates. Uber is losing money at the rate of about $2 billion a year; delivery platforms like Foodora and Deliveroo are also operating at a loss (but not Uber Eats, which is the only part of the Uber concern to make any money). These meagre earnings are threatened by growing labour protests among platform workers and by substantial 'regulatory risks' as organized taxis and hotels, along with neighbourhood associations resisting Airbnb-led gentrification, are fighting back.[31] One gets the feeling that, more than real earnings potential, these platforms are kept alive by large financial actors that find very little else to invest in. After all, Facebook, Uber and

Silicon Valley start-ups are about all that remains of US tech innovation, and they cannot be allowed to fail. But neither are they particularly attractive as investments. And this realization is now dawning on the venture capital system as a whole. Ploughing billions of dollars into the search for a handful of unicorns simply does not make much economic sense.[32]

The whole system has come to resemble a Ponzi scheme where earnings take the form of additional capital gains rather than sustainable market revenue. But even as a Ponzi scheme, the start-up/venture capital system does not perform that well. Then average returns to venture capital funds have more or less followed the S&P index, albeit with much higher volatility. So, as a whole, the system is not able to make more money from 'new tech' than what can be made from 'old tech', under much more secure conditions. This poor performance is reflected in the transformation of the start-up acceleration business. As the recent boom in start-up investments begin to level out, accelerators are diversifying away from their original business – start-up acceleration – that has proved less profitable than expected. In 2016 only 77 out of 579 Accelerator programmes worldwide reported that they had an exit. In total, there were 178 exits worldwide, out of 11,305 start-ups. In fact, in 2015, with the exception of Africa and the Middle East, the traditional 'cash-for-equity' model, first established by Y-Combinator, which involves investing a small amount of seed money in a start-up – around $25,000 on average – in exchange for equity (usually between 5% and 10%) is being abandoned. To quote the 2016 Global Accelerator Report, by no means a critical forum:

> Increasingly, this model is becoming rare, as more accelerators reconsider their general outlook. Most likely, the small number of exits – 178 reported in 2016 – has proven insufficient in funding their operations. Consequently, many accelerators around the world no longer rely on generating revenue from exits. Accelerators have relied on, and continue to explore, new models of revenue generation. 90.4% of accelerators plan to increase their revenue in the medium to long term by incorporating alternative revenue models in addition to exits. 52.1% of accelerators are at least partially

funded by a corporation, and 67.2% aim to generate future revenue from services sold to corporations.[33]

The figures give the impression that the main response on the part of industrial capitalism is unable to provide economic sustainability to the new industriousness. True, the venture capital start-up system has created a number of useful service platforms with a global or almost global reach, but they do not appear to be economically sustainable, neither for the workers who produce the services on which these platforms are supposed to thrive, nor for the investors. Overall the 'winner take all' model on which they build appears to be overly wasteful with regard to the creativity that resides in the new industriousness: innovation, far from being disruptive, is standardized and tends to become more of the same. Above all, the capitalist response is marked by a fundamental lack of ideas or perspectives. Start-ups are encouraged to repeat established ideas, and platforms propose business models that seek to rationalize some minor aspects of an established industrial consumer society that remains in essence unchanged (pizza delivery via app, instead of simply calling up the local pizzeria). They testify to the inability of the remains of industrial capitalism to imagine a future substantially different from the present.

A Chinese cycle of accumulation?

However inefficient in its present state, the unicorn model does point towards a new model of capitalist accumulation. The start-up economy and the platform economies are both attempts to use new forms of algorithmic control to standardize industrious activity and transform it into a predictable source of income and, importantly, financial rent. In this way, contemporary digital capitalism responds to an accelerating popular industriousness through a combination of mass industriousness and top–down despotic control. In its Silicon Valley version, this approach never became truly effective, either as a source of really disruptive innovation or as a series of highly profitable business ventures. At least in part this is due to the fact that the Silicon Valley paradigm of 'disruptive innovation' masks a fundamental lack of attention to real social needs. From its very inception, Silicon Valley has been guided by an engineering approach where technological possibility can translate into business ventures with little concern for the social desirability of the outcome, much less attention to the overall social model in which such innovations might operate. This approach is reflected in the wasteful logic of venture capital, where money is 'thrown at' start-ups without paying serious attention to their usefulness and where, consequently, business success is reduced to a problem of statistical probability. It is also reflected in the conservative nature of the contemporary platform economy, where the new technology is used primarily to appropriate and transform existing markets or services.

However, this model might become the core of a new cycle of Chinese capitalism. Unlike US actors, Chinese digital companies together with the Chinese state are implementing digital platforms and venture investments with an overall social and economic strategy in mind. Digital e-commerce platforms, digital payment systems and investments in micro-enterprises aim to generate 'mass innovation and entrepreneurship', particularly in rural areas. Connecting to markets via Alibaba's Taobao platform, so-called 'Taobao villages' have generated 37 million jobs based on small-scale industrious enterprise. Similar programmes combining e-commerce platforms, small-scale venture investments and the re-discovery of traditional agricultural techniques aim at transforming parts of the Chinese agricultural sector into an industrious economy based on small enterprises, locally specific agricultural techniques and a re-appropriation of centuries-old forms of 'village rationality'.[34]

At the other end of this spectrum, China is a world leader in developing new despotic control systems using digital data and surveillance algorithms. These are used for a multitude of purposes, from evaluating worker performance to predicting urban crowd behaviour and, importantly, estimating credit scores on the bases of more or less virtuous patterns of online and consumer behaviour. Indeed, access to microcredit for small-scale business ventures is dependent on scorings of overall 'citizenship virtue'. This model is set to expand geographically as Chinese digital platforms follow the Belt and Road initiative for economic expansion into Central Asia.[35]

The combination of an economic base of small-scale industrious production and top–down despotic control via algorithms and platforms strongly resembles the model of Chinese imperial political economy established already in the Ming period, prior to the Great Divergence that effectively set the West apart from the rest. Its return would entail a new cycle of accumulation based on what in effect would be a partial reversal to pre-capitalist relations of production. Capitalist accumulation would depend on the ability to tax a large multitude of small-scale industrious producers that each produce very little in terms of value added. It would operate in an authoritarian and conservative fashion, through a state-centred omnipresent 'control society'.[36]

Such a Chinese cycle of accumulation would be more efficient than the Silicon Valley version of digital capitalism that we are seeing today, in that it would be able to expand markets for digitally enabled industriousness through attention to genuinely popular needs and desires. (Indeed, Chinese venture capital investments in artificial intelligence (AI) and consumer robotics have already dwarfed those of US funds.) However, it would also remain inherently conservative. It would be based on low profit margins and on gradual piecemeal innovation adapting new technologies to popular needs. It would remain locked into an imaginary that privileges continuous economic growth (however slow) within an established consumerist model. It would also require continuous repression of the kinds of technological and social innovations that might point towards alternative arrangements. Most importantly, it would eventually run into insuperable ecological barriers, in the form of resource and energy scarcity.

Industrious anti-capitalism

To be able to do something that is meaningful and true to one's values, while at the same time surviving by selling the resulting produce on the market is the most common desire that inspires the new industrious economy. The aim is mostly not profit maximization, but a situation in which talents can find an equitable or just value on markets that are democratic and transparent. The universal vision to accompany contemporary industrious modernity, at least among its main 'carrying group' of entrepreneurial knowledge workers, is a kind of petty commodity exchange where social media campaigns can be exchanged for locally made craft gin, or ecologically conscious fashion clothes. Consequently, a large share of the projects that emerge out of the start-up and social enterprise scene are attempts to create such just and transparent markets: crowdfunding solutions that enable ethically virtuous companies to attract capital from a large crowd of small-scale investors; online platforms that sell clothes from designers with low ecological impact, or wines from growers that show particular devotion and passion; apps that match social enterprises with ethical investors, blockchain applications that ensure traceability and transparency without the need for central control. Similar to the guilds and commercial fraternities that were forming in European cities in the High Middle Ages, digital entrepreneurship is accompanied by attempts to create and structure markets according to communitarian ideas of fairness and ethics. And digital technologies have made a significant contribution to this task of bottom-up market-making.

Among industrious knowledge workers, most of these attempts are inspired, at least to some extent, by notions of sharing, openness or peer production. Not all embrace this vision in full, but most draw on some aspect of it, at least in principle. (Even a corporate behemoth like Facebook is about sharing, connecting and being 'social'.) Some even suggest that we are witnessing the emergence of a new 'mode of production' distinct from both socialism and capitalism. Such commons-based peer production (CBPP) is characterized by the suspension of both market exchange and central planning in favour of decentralized sharing. Inspired by Nobel laureate Elinor Ostrom's work, these theories suggest that the commons come with new forms of communitarian governance, where productive efforts as well as the goods that result from them are shared according to egalitarian norms and principles. Different from both bureaucratic state power and the exchange logic of the market, the commons are governed by communities. To some, this entails a new definition of value that reflects the irreducible diversity of particular local contexts and communities. To quote David Bollier, on the commons, each of the different 'world-making communities', be these 'community theater, open-source microscopy, open-source mapping to aid humanitarian rescue and hospitality for migrants' are 'animated by their own values, traditions, history and intersubjectivity'. To others, the new commons-based economy simply entails a suspension of the question of value. Yochai Benkler suggests that CBPP signals the dawn of a new age of 'social sharing' and redistribution. In short, CBPP is more than a way to organize the creation of valuable things; it has the potential to realize a new redistributive economic system as well as an attempt to 'rescue the messy realities of human existence and social organization from the faux regularities and worldview of standard economics, bureaucratic systems and modernity itself'.[37]

In its strongest form, this vision is offering a revitalization of the social movements of the Left. It informs a significant global social movement, the 'commons movement', where 'commonism' is understood as an alternative both to capitalism and to a universalizing modernity – the institutional basis for a new decentralized global society made up of a plurality of diverse self-governing communities. Commonism has also been an influential inspiration for the multitude of movements that fight for the preservation of traditional commons and the associated lifestyles, often more advanced and rational than the 'modern' alternatives, at least from an ecological point of view. Here the commons represent not just a new 'asset class' (to use a perhaps excessively crude economic term) but, also 'a new way of looking at the world, one that opens up the competitive, mechanistic, profit-centric mindset that has ruled Western civilization since the dawn of the Industrial Revolution, with a more humanistic, environmentally aware and holistic world view'.[38]

There are a number of projects that attempt to translate this vision into reality and realize an institutional framework for such a commons-based economy. Community-based agricultural projects proliferate in what is known as the 'new food economy'. More radical co-working spaces form new guild-like organizations and practise revenue sharing. Blockchain-based alternative currencies seek to realize local economies that are democratically governed and informed by alternative value systems.[39] However, few are able to do away with markets entirely.

Or, rather, sharing without exchange and reciprocity operates well at the level of production. But this is not really new. Already in Marx's analysis of nineteenth-century factories, collaboration and the sharing of knowledge and other resources emerged as an intrinsic aspect of the factory-based capitalist mode of production. This collaborative aspect has been increased in the digitized economy, and in particular in the forms of digitized knowledge work that supports most (if not all) of the initiatives informed by the vision of commonism. However, very few examples rely exclusively on sharing as a form of distribution. (Indeed, one could argue that knowledge, skills and other resources that are prone to digitalization can be freely shared because being *common*, they have very little value. What is not shared, but instead jealously guarded and cultivated in these communities, is reputation, which instead is scarce and valuable.) Most of these communities, even the most self-consciously commonist ones, rather rely on some combination of market exchange with the endorsement of commonist and sharing-oriented values, and, when applicable, more democratic forms of market governance.

Indeed, most attempts to institutionalize a commons-based value logic build on some form of exchange. A significant number of projects within the commonist movement consist in attempts at creating commons-based markets, that is, forms of market exchange that transpire within a system of norms, values and legal frameworks or algorithmic structures that are themselves determined, in some way, by participants in a commons-based community, or by collaboration between several such communities. The alternative food economy is rich with similar initiatives, perhaps because the tangible reality of material produce facilitates market exchange. Lately also the 'sharing economy' has seen a proliferation of 'platform cooperatives', that is, platforms for market exchange – similar to those of Uber and Airbnb – that operate algorithmic matching of supply and demand, but that are, crucially, owned, controlled and operated by their users. On these platforms the rules of market exchange are inscribed in the software of the platform, including its matching algorithms. These rules have been decided and can be changed through some form of members' co-governance structures. Within the framework of these rules, market exchange occurs and money is regularly exchanged for goods and services. Blockchain-based technologies offer off-the-shelf solutions for building similar platform cooperatives with a minimum of effort in programming and design. Some of these platforms, like Enspiral or Sensorica, are networks of social entrepreneurs and similar projects that share work as well as revenue collectively – in the case of Enspiral, physically located in a co-working space. Sensorica also operates a sophisticated value accounting infrastructure that calculates the value accumulated by particular users, which then translates into their share of the overall monetary profits accumulated by the particular project to which they have contributed. Many co-working spaces are experimenting with similar internal commons-based markets. Similar forms of commons-based exchange value are proliferating as blockchain technologies are making it significantly simpler to launch alternative currencies. Here, too, the idea is to create institutionally supported systems of exchange that take into account notions of value that have been determined by participants in some form of collective deliberation, and that successively enable their efforts to be exchanged according to some principle of equivalence. While the principle here is to re-appropriate the value produced by social cooperation, this re-appropriation is nevertheless achieved through market-like forms of exchange.[40]

Even within strongly *commonist* organizations, like free software communities or even Wikipedia, the ideology of sharing is implemented, at a practical level, through markets or market-like mechanisms. Most of these organizations operate with some kind of reputation systems, where individual contributions are collectively valued, and where those valuations, implicit or, increasingly, also explicit can be used as personal social capital, able to attract and mobilize participation or, often, be transferred to other communities or even monetized on the mainstream professional market. A good reputation in the Debian community, for example, translates into power and influence within the community, making it easier to initiate projects and mobilize other members for one's ideas. It is also a significant asset on the job market, facilitating access to programmer 'gigs' and raising the market value of one's skills. Often such reputations are made explicit in the form of ratings, 'stars' and scores of various kinds. Indeed, in a survey of more than 300 peer-production communities, about three-quarters of the communities asked used some form of internal evaluation system. And in the ethnographic fieldwork that accompanied the survey, the desire to quantify, and above all to quantify in ways that were more rational and more transparent and that enabled exchange between communities, was one of the more frequent issues that we encountered. Even in its most ideologically conscious, its most *commonist* part, the overall direction of the emerging industrious economy seems not to be the downright refusal of exchange value and markets in the interest of safeguarding the differences and particularities of the local value system. Instead, it is the construction of new forms of exchange value that have been created in more democratic ways and that, above all, reflect and render transferable the virtue of members in contributing to constructing and empowering such specific local communities. Rather than a movement that seeks to do away with markets, *commonism*, in practice at least, seeks to take control of market exchange and subsume it under communitarian principles of value that often go beyond the merely economic.

However, even as they embrace market exchange in practice, available figures show that earnings for these projects are usually far from sufficient to guarantee sustainability. In a survey of the alternative agriculture sector in Southern Italy, only about a third of the organizations that we interacted with were able to support themselves from their activities. Almost half earned close to nothing at all (indeed, recourse to alternative forms of exchange like barter occurred quite frequently). Similarly, a survey of participants in peer-production communities indicate that few were able to make a living from the activity that they were most passionate about, while a full 60 per cent saw their participation in these communities as a complement to less passionate, but more remunerative 'day jobs'. Taobao fashion designers, even the more successful ones, earn in the range of €200–500 per month. Rates of success in the start-up economy along with various freelancer scenes confirm these observations. While the prospect of a spectacular 'exit' or the achievement of commercially profitable Instafame looms as a universal *mirage*, the reality for most people in the industrious economy is that the ideal of passionate petty commodity production runs into a reality where market sustainability is a major problem.[41]

Often the only way in which such sustainability can be achieved is by interacting with corporate capital or the state. Maker spaces, although aspiring to create an alternative market for small-scale, high-tech artisans, are often forced to rely on corporate consulting or the provision of seminars or 'experiences' for corporate clients as a means of survival. Freelancing creatives in co-working spaces, while desiring to engage in egalitarian petty commodity exchange with their peers, depended mostly on commissions from large corporate clients. Social enterprises prosper in cities like London, where multinational corporations spend their corporate social responsibility budgets. Indeed, the success of industrious entrepreneurs seems to largely depend on the outsourcing of a growing number of corporate services, or more generally of the reproduction of the cultural and lifestyle conditions for a viable investment environment. Sharing economy initiatives are financed by city governments, or increasingly by investors as part of attempts to create an urban environment that valorizes real-estate investments. The industrious economy is thus assuming the same role as the 'creative economy' did a decade ago. Like the informal or semi-formal economy of taxi drivers, pizza makers, drug dealers and prostitutes that began to grow in globalizing cities like London or New York three decades ago, the contemporary hipster economy is part of the provision of diversified services that is central to processes of gentrification. In the end, this 'hipster economy' of craft butchers and bartenders depends on the presence of a mass of high-paid corporate employees that can purchase its services.

However, there are signs that more sustainable forms of autonomous markets might be emerging. At the bottom level of global supply chains, the pirate or Shanzhai economy has enabled sustainable alternative value circuits for more than a decade. The pirate economy, a direct epiphenomenon of the outsourcing of production and the subsequent becoming common of skills and knowledge, has grown dramatically in the last decades, and has radically improved its technological capacity. The Chinese Shanzhai system represented an integration of the knowledge commons of the global pirate economy with those of the dense electronic manufacturing districts that had formed around the Pearl River Delta. This integration supported an autonomous value circuit where profits and money can flow outside of the official capitalist economy using traditional Chinese social network-based financing and informal money transfers. Shanzhai also developed its own aesthetic, cheap and cheerful, ironic and disrespectful towards the identitarian aesthetic of dominant brands (to the extent that Shanzhai was saluted in Chinese popular culture as a symbol of popular rebellion). The Shanzhai system has since lost influence, partly on account of repression on the part of the Chinese government, partly because the politics of planned obsolescence of Apple and Samsung products has generated a large supply of used, but still functional branded smartphones for which there is a popular second-hand market. At the same time, the organizational and technical solutions that Shanzhai pioneered has inspired a new generation of Chinese quality brands like Xiaomi that uses its supply chains and employs many of its designers and manufacturers.[42] For some time, however, Shanzhai exemplified a functioning non-capitalist market, based on small-scale industrious producers, making do by rapidly responding to the real needs of consumers. It did not come with the overall visions for social transformation that instead prevail in the commons movements. Shanzhai entrepreneurs rather exposed a 'brash get-rich-quick mentality and a cynical embrace of market competition'.[43] Today Shenzhen is populated with industrious knowledge workers in the many hardware incubators that now proliferate there, and who use overcapacity in the small factories that used to be part of Shanzhai networks for product prototyping.

Even as the geographical distance between the material and immaterial aspects of industrious commodity production have been reduced, substantial cultural differences remain between the two 'scenes'. However, this gap is set to narrow as former Shanzhai manufacturers are increasingly embracing immaterial aspects of the production process, getting into marketing and design and not simply manufacturing.[44] The convergence of productivity levels is also set to narrow the gap as we are witnessing something akin to a class recomposition, where knowledge workers are getting poorer at the same time as material producers are seeing a technological upgrade. Immaterial and material producers in the industrious economy might increasingly find themselves 'in the same boat', and perhaps begin to articulate a common vision of an industrious future.

At the same time, the bourgeois knowledge worker part of the industrious economy is seeing the emergence of similar autonomous value circuits. Starting with blockchain, the growing 'crypto' or token economy is enabling entrepreneurs to raise capital and pay collaborators without having to pass through the official venture capital system. In 2017, blockchain-based start-ups have raised $7 billion by means of so-called ICOs or initial coin offerings. In 2018, that figured reached $21 billion. These effectively constitute an alternative market for capital often based, in part, on pooling resources from a large multitude of small-scale 'retail' investors, many of whom have themselves earned their money from blockchain-related investments. (ICO trading is in effect banned in a number of countries, including China.) While many ICOs are speculative, and some downright fraudulent, overall the new 'token economy' is directed towards financing investments in building a new alternative infrastructure for economic transactions, legal registers and new forms of productive collaborations. For example, DAOs (or distributed autonomous organizations – a sort of automatic managerial protocols) can contribute to creating alternative global supply chains by radically reducing the costs involved in managing such processes. Community token economics have facilitated the maintenance of 'value sovereignty', enabling a community of producers to stay on the market while maintaining greater control over the motivations that structure participation on the part of their members. Community protocols like holochain make possible 'a social operating system' that is both faster and less energy consuming than blockchains. At the same time, the token economy and the community finance system that it has enabled has also enabled new forms of remuneration for collaborators. Blockchain-based projects are rich in cash, also the non-corporate ones, and they are hiring collaborators, not only programmers but also people who can communicate, design interfaces, write white papers, etc. By being paid in crypto currencies, these collaborators are able to maintain a sustainable standard of living, while at the same time escaping the bureaucracy, the humiliating pitches and motivational seminars and all the other nonsense that comes with participation in the official venture capital system. Most of its participants see it as an alternative to, or even an escape from, a venture capital system that has lost most of its legitimacy.[45]

Conclusion

Industrious relations of production have developed as an effect of capitalist restructuring. Successively, the new commons resulting from capitalist globalization have been appropriated and used in the development of a series of market-based economic circuits that partly operate outside of, and often are framed as opposed or alternative to, the 'true' capitalist economy. Capitalism has adapted to this new commons-based industriousness chiefly by developing a unicorn economy able to harvest mass industriousness and transform it into financial rent. In its US version, this is not very efficient, but a return of the long delegitimized notion of an Asiatic mode of production, in the form of a Chinese-centred regime of accumulation, might make this model sustainable, at least in the short run.

There also signs that the new industrious precariat are escaping from their subsumption under corporate supply chains, platforms or venture capital and starting to re-appropriate the new commons at their disposal in the form of alternative value circuits. To date, the economically most significant of these has emerged at the bottom end of global supply chains, where the pirate economy has created independent forms of appropriation of the general intellect created in corporate supply chains. Today, we are seeing similar developments in the knowledge worker part of the industrious economy, as blockchain applications and other technologies are enabling autonomous organizational forms and the bottom-up creation of markets and financial circuits in ways that were difficult to imagine only a decade ago. This might very well lead to an empowerment of the industrious economy vis-à-vis what is left of industrial capitalism, in particular as it acquires its own financial and economic circuits, and thereby, at least is in part able to create its own value forms. In the process we are likely to see a convergence between the bourgeois and the proletarian part of the industrious economy. This might lead to a greater focus on actual use values. Until now, the knowledge worker part of the industrious economy has developed ideological visions of a new kind of petty commodity exchange based on ethically grounded use values. But its distance from markets and its dependence on corporate or venture capital, family support or other kinds of welfare, has meant that notions of value often remain linked to aloof and largely unrealistic ideas of individual self-realization, technological 'disruption' or large-scale social transformation. Such convergence might also lead to a skills and technology upgrade of the already organizationally efficient global pirate economy. This has the potential to generate new innovation in the face of a rapidly declining industrial capitalism. (Will the needs of tomorrow's food economy be met by organizations like RuralHack that develop cheap and accessible farm machinery based on Open Source technologies; by back-alley Shanzhai entrepreneurs equipped with $1,000 systems for genetic editing like CRISPR, or by corporate behemoths like Monsanto?) In the process, the current political programme that ranges from a return to classical liberalism to a naïve embrace of anarcho-libertarianism might grow more realistic and grounded, and the solutionism that the anti-capitalist commons share with their Silicon Valley nemesis might be moderated by a more careful attention to the actual complexities of social and political institutions. It is unlikely, however, that this will lead to a head-on confrontation with the capitalist 'system'. Rather than the radical and heroic revolutions that first come to mind when we think of the origins of industrial modernity, the process looks more like the slower and more gradual industrious revolution that prepared the way for European modernity since, arguably, the turn of the second millennium.

5

A New Industrious Revolution?

The capitalist mode of production that appeared trium-
phant at the 'end of history' only thirty years ago has run
out of ideas for the future. Despite grandiose celebrations
of 'disruptive' technologies and businesses ideas, innovation
is slowing and contemporary capitalism is unable to evolve
beyond its twentieth-century industrial version. We are still
stuck with a system based on wasteful mass production
for equally wasteful mass consumption. Most innovations,
from Facebook to artificial intelligence, operate on the
premise that things remain that way. Social media companies
envision that they can keep making their money from selling
advertising; AI is marketed as a technology apt at fine-tuning
Amazon purchases and selecting ambient playlists for the
suburban home. The technological acceleration that has
come with digital connectivity appears to be but a surface
phenomenon. In German sociologist Hartmut Rosa's words,
we find ourselves in a 'fundamental historical rigidity in
which nothing essential changes anymore, however rapidly
things may alter on the surface'.[1]

Intellectuals seem particularly incapable of envisioning
a future for our times. Silicon Valley pundits suggest that
we are now reaching a 'singularity' beyond which nothing
can be known (which is just another, quasi-religious, way
of saying that you don't have a clue!). Alternatively, they

suggest that we go to Mars, where presumably we would build a replica of Palo Alto with the very same corporate campuses, shopping centres and Starbucks coffee houses. The Left is stuck in scholastic debates on identity politics or alternatively seems to be waiting for a magic re-ignition of the old social movements of industrial modernity. But our times are not ripe for revolution, at least not yet. And the Age of Revolutions that brought in industrial modernity is not the right model for understanding the potential of contemporary change.[2]

Instead, we might need to go further back to find a model for the transformation ahead of us: the transition *to* capitalism that marked Europe in the long sixteenth century (*ca* 1450–1650). Like our immediate future, that transition was marked by wars, social upheavals and environmental disaster. Like in our times the transition was driven by a new stratum of small-scale industrious producers who saw the expansion of markets as a foundation for a new freer and more modern social order ('free speech and free trade', as the petition of the Levellers demanded in 1653). In this chapter, I will briefly review the story of this European transition, and the 'industrious revolution' that drove it, in order to look at our immediate future from a different point of view.[3]

As this book has suggested many times before, the experience of 'modernity', the sensation that we can 'change the world', is older than its industrial version, which we have come to know in the nineteenth and twentieth centuries. To Max Weber, modernity was pioneered in the sixteenth century, by the puritans. It was the followers of Calvin, Baxter and to a lesser extent Luther, and later the Pietists, the Methodists and the American Baptists and Quakers who broke with the status quo of traditional society and proposed a new ethics based on continuous work and improvement, first in economic life, and subsequently in all aspects of social existence. Weber suggests that the puritans were the unintentional harbingers of the 'spirit of modern capitalism', the impetus to continuous work and improvement that would become the main engine of the modernization process. Weber's puritans preceded the industrial revolution. They contributed to bringing it about even if they might not have planned to do so.[4] However, Weber recognized that some elements of what was to become the protestant ethic had earlier origins. As his contemporary Werner Sombart pointed out, an emphasis on industriousness and frugality, basic elements of economic rationally and a notion that the individual had a responsibility to intervene in the world and act on it, were present in some streams of medieval monastic thought, and in the writings of Italian thirteenth-century humanists like Leon Battista Alberti and Bernardino of Siena. These notions were also to be found in the many treatises on business or household administration that flourished in the period. The puritans drew on these elements, as well as many others, notably the tradition of alchemy and 'natural magic' that saw a revival in the sixteenth and seventeenth centuries, to articulate a modern ethic of inner worldly industriousness, of working hard for a calling in order to change the world.[5] However, let us follow Sombart's thread for a while. It shows how elements of what we have called an 'industrious modernity' played an important role in the growth and ensuing collapse of European feudalism, in ways not entirely unlike what seems to be unfurling today.

The first industrious revolution

British historian Robert I. Moore locates the origins of the modern world to what he calls the 'first European revolution' at the turn of the second millennium, which he suggests signified the first real exit from the world of antiquity. In Europe at that time, the Church was revitalized by the new monastic orders and formed an alliance with the 'little people' to contain the anarchic violence that resulted from the collapse of the Carolingian Empire. 'Evil men who had sprung up like weeds, seized the goods and animals of the poor, holding them to ransom and forcing them to work, especially on building the castles from which the usurpers imposed this reign of terror on the countryside.'[6] With the reassertion of royal power in the eleventh century, this 'Peace Movement' built an alliance between a revitalized church and the 'little people'. It was informed by a new religious fervour centred on relics and monastic preachers. Eventually it became an important factor in the institutionalization of feudalism as a legal and morally regulated social order with its checks and balances, and with the Church as its spiritual and moral authority.

This was also the time of a revival of commerce and communication across Western Europe and in particular Italy and Flanders, and the growth of towns. Economic historian Robert Lopez calls this the 'medieval commercial revolution'. Population increase revitalized the countryside and 'changed the face of Europe' from a sparsely populated continent with immense woods to a network of towns and villages similar to what we can see today in the countryside of Italy or France. Growing agricultural productivity created a greater surplus to feed a growing population in better ways. Lopez refers to how residents of a beggars' hospice in Tuscany in 765 lived on a daily ration of 'one measure of bread, two measures of wine and two servings of a thick gruel made of beans and millet and seasoned with olive oil'. The residents of a similar structure in Champagne in 1325 had instead 'meat three times a week as well as eggs, herrings and bread, oil, salt and onions'.[7] Higher population density, better living standards and improved communication – travel grew less risky as social order was reasserted in the eleventh century – supported the growth of commerce and of towns and markets. This commercial expansion was also an effect of the affirmation of the Italian merchant cities: Venice, Florence, Genoa and Pisa. The Italian merchants built on pre-existing ties with the eastern Mediterranean. They exploited these connections to construct a trading network that spanned from 'Greenland to Beijing'. It connected France, England and the Netherlands, where Italian traders controlled the money-lending business and most of the trade in wool, wine, grain and other basic agricultural commodities, with the eastern Mediterranean and, via the Genoese presence on the coasts of the Black Sea, the Silk Road to China. This network brought spices, silk and luxuries from Asia to wealthy consumers in Europe, wool from England to the manufacturing centres of Flanders, Picardy and Lombardy; wine and agricultural produce from Southern to Northern Europe, among many other things. It significantly reduced the risk of famine by securing a constant supply of grain.

The Italian trading network was supported by a new financial infrastructure allowing merchants to issue letters of credit and cash them in the many offices of Italian moneylenders (*banche*) to be found from London to Cairo. It built on regular communications: there was a weekly courier service that connected Italian cities to the fairs of Champagne and letters and documents were transported across a Mediterranean Sea that 'was now full of ships'.[8] The expansion of the Italian 'world economy' created growing wealth in the thirteenth century, principally in Italy, which at the time was the commercial centre of Europe, but also in the manufacturing centres of northwestern Europe and in England. The intensification of commercial activity and communication and – to use a quaint term found in many old translations of Karl Marx – 'intercourse among men' led to four important developments that would be crucial for the European modernization process that followed: the growth of towns; the development of commons; the emergence of a new stratum of industrious pretty producers who relied on the commons in order to make a living; and an ideological outlook centred on new ideas of freedom, individuality and the value of industrious work along with the notion that the world could be changed according to the plans and ideas of human actors.

Driven by trade, manufacturing and improved communications, Europe went through a first period of urbanization from about 1000 until the arrival of the Black Death in the second half of the fourteenth century. Towns were centres of commerce as well as of new ideas and new kinds of freedom. They attracted former serfs who had fled the countryside or had been kicked out by feudal land reclamations, along with dispossessed knights, children of the minor nobility left without an inheritance, wandering clerics and other varieties of the 'masterless men' who began to be a permanent feature of a European continent in transformation. In the towns they could engage in trade or commerce, or in labour-intensive artisan petty production as an alternative to the mercenary adventures or brigandage that, at least for the nobility, had been the main alternative before. Gradually the cities came to rival the fairs as centres for commercial activity. In Northern Italy, the towns acquired independence, came to absorb most of the local minor nobility and dominate the surrounding countryside. (At the Battle of Legnano in 1176, the cities of Northern Italy gained effective, if not formal, independence from the Holy Roman Emperor Frederick Barbarossa.) In the rest of Europe their degrees of independence varied, but most feudal seigneurs understood the advantage of lifting restrictions on trade and refraining from excessive taxation.[9]

The towns also became a centre for the creation of new ideas and lifestyles. The cities were the focus for the many 'millenarian movements' that flourished in Europe. Inspired by utopian visions like those of Joachim of Fiore and later the emerging Franciscan movement, a multitude of preachers congregated their followers – dispossessed peasants, runaway serfs, disbanded mercenaries, exploited artisan apprentices – in cities where they demanded justice and equality in the here and now. In the cities even the poor began to develop a new outlook on life. Formal equality and the fortunes of the market made it possible to nurture visions of a more meritocratic and individualistic society. Rising standards of living and the proliferation of new luxury goods created new wants and desires, even among those who did not have the means to satisfy them. As Norman Cohn writes of the new category of 'masterless men', living at the margins of the new urban civilization:

> There were however many who merely acquired new wants without being able to satisfy them; and in them the spectacle of a wealth undreamt-of in earlier centuries provoked a bitter sense of frustration. In all the over-populated, relatively urbanized and industrialized areas there were many people living on the margin of society, in a state of chronic insecurity. There industry even at the best of times could never absorb the whole of the surplus population.[10]

The towns also became centres for a revitalized intellectual life. Wealthy merchants, as well as a growing public administration supported artists and intellectuals who were awarded new degrees of freedom in relation to the Church. At the same time guilds and corporations, formed by merchants and artisans, had not yet transformed into the stalwarts for progress that they would appear to be to eighteenth-century liberals, but were at least sometimes 'living labs' for the creation of new organizational and legal forms, like the new accounting systems that developed in the thirteenth century, as well as new outlooks and philosophies. Often the guilds supported the new universities that nurtured intellectuals and worked to develop new legal forms like the *lex mercatorium* that regulated the conduct of merchants and, by extension, the whole population of the towns. The rising importance of the *lex mercatorium* in relation to the tradition of Roman law or the Ecclesiastic Law that had developed in the High Middle Ages was reflected in the more tolerant attitudes towards usury that developed during the thirteenth and fourteenth centuries. Towns, with their guilds, universities and wealthy merchants grew to rival the church and the monasteries as centres for intellectual life and their freer, more individualistic and hedonistic (at least in aspiration) lifestyles also became the centres for a new tradition of 'humanist' thought. This could be religious, as in the pious preaching of Albertanus of Brescia, a member of the legal corporation in Brescia, a graduate of the University of Bologna and, after a brief period of incarceration, *assessor* or high-level civil servant in Genoa until his disappearance from the records in 1253. Or it could be blatantly secular, as in the songs of Sienese poet adventurer Cecco Angiolieri celebrating a new kind of hedonistic individualism. At the heart of this tradition stood an orientation towards worldly life, either in Albertanus's admonition that 'God loves an industrious man' or in Angiolieri's invitations to drink and be merry. The humanist intellectuals were expressions of a secular tradition that, in Italian economic historian Oscar Nuccio's perhaps excessively polemical words, anticipated Weber's puritans by 'at least four centuries'. This humanist tradition was later to be partially incorporated in Franciscan economic thought and inspire institutions like the Monte di pietà or the rural equivalent the Monte Frummentari, a sort of sharing economy *ante literam* that sought to combine economic rationality and markets with solidarity and civic duty. It contained an affirmation of economic rationality as a natural state of man – an orientation that Weber would call 'inner worldly', that is the idea that God's work is better furthered by industrious activity than by contemplation and prayer, and a vision that combined economic activity with peaceful and just civic life.[11] The institution of the commons was central to this new social vision.

The medieval commons

In the country the demographic upswing and growth of trade created increased pressure on land and other natural resources. As this continued, arable land became scarce, and as a consequence the pressure to convert forest and pasture increased. In part, this came from natural limits to agricultural productivity. In part, it resulted from seigneurial attempts to increase rent extraction. The centralization of power at royal courts meant that local rural seigneurs, just like the emerging bourgeoise of the towns, began to aspire to more expensive consumption styles, now a necessity at court. At the same time, an expanding commercial activity led to declining relative value of land rents vis-à-vis commercial profits. As Jean Birrell sees the process in an article on the English forest commons in the thirteenth century:

> Increased population pressure in the 13th century, the growth of towns and increase in demand and in trade produced a pressure on resources, which was sometimes acute. In particular, shortage of arable land led to the asserting of marginal land often at the expense of pastures and clearance of woodland. At the same time seigneurial pressure on the peasantry was stepped up, as lords of manors attempted to maintain their incomes in the face of rising prices and the attractions of a higher standard of living and in doing so took advantage of their power over a numerous and often impoverished peasantry.[12]

This and similar processes led to a cycle of peasant struggles where traditional common rights were defended and, when successful, codified and made explicit in new ways, and where new ones were introduced. The resulting *commons*, often highly complicated arrangements of varying rights of access, could be seen as 'settlements of conflicts that arose between the lords and the inhabitants of a village' that developed in the context of the 'great European reclamations that took place during the tenth to the twelfth centuries'. Sometimes this process included the inscription of some of these settlements into law, as in the case of the English Magna Carta and the accompanying Forest Charter of 1225. In other words, the commons arose as part of a new feudal 'settlement' – as a crucial institution that in turn resulted from a new intensity in communication, trade and 'social intercourse' more generally. The rural commons were crucial to the village economy, ensuring the reproduction of labour power. At the same time, they became a focus for peasant struggles against feudal repression and increasingly against the enclosures and other attempts at land reclamations that followed on the commercialization of agriculture.[13]

The urban guilds that flourished in the same period sprung out of the new social environment of the growing cities. Along with fraternities and religious orders, guilds provided a space where new identities and rule systems could be articulated. This would serve to regulate and improve productive and commercial activities and, importantly, reduce insecurity. This applied in an economic sense as guilds were able to fix prices, set the rules of market exchange and provide a number of welfare services for their members. It also applied in an existential sense as, like the new monastic orders, guilds provided a meaningful framework for life, endowing it with goals and aims, along with the secrets and rituals that were able to enforce them. And while the guilds certainly functioned to protect against the risks of the market, they also supported the development of a new market society. They did this by regulating market transactions, but also by providing a source of social capital and class identity for merchants and artisans – thus contributing to altering their status.[14]

It might be justified to distinguish between the emergence of the rural commons mainly as reactions to intensified exploitation, and the emergence of the urban guilds as institutionalizations of a new more 'modern' relational modality typical of an early market society. However, the picture is not that simple. The urban guilds many times rose to defend petty producers from both seigneurial pressure and the pressure from city governments. They often took the side of the oppressed in important social struggles, such as the revolt of the artisan guilds in Ghent, or that of the Ciompi in Florence in 1378.

Conversely the rural commons were also to some extent an effect of the marketization of rural society. This applied in the sense of the penetration of market relations into the countryside that favoured new forms of free association and facilitated the cooperation between village communities. It also applied in the sense of the emergence of a new 'rural middle class' that used the commons as a resource for market participation and in affirming their position against that of feudal lords. As historian John Maddicott describes the role of the new English gentry in enforcing the Magna Carta in the thirteenth century,

> [In this period] we for the first time see the emergence of the gentry of the shires as a political force. [...] In the thirteenth century their authority and cohesion was enhanced by a nexus of more recent social and legal changes. The rise of the knights as an administrative class, the growth of the freedom to alienate and inherit land, which gradually emancipated them together with their tenants from the bonds of feudal lordship, the permeability of the boundary between knights and freeholders, which maintained the privileged position of the freeholder, once the *villein* had lost access to the royal courts. These changes worked to produce a society in which the ties of neighbourhood mattered as much as those of lordship. They helped create the gentry, which embraced more than the relatively small elite of knights who headed it and which was sharply sensitive to local needs and interests.[15]

In the cities and in the countryside the guilds and the commons supported the development of a new middle class of industrious 'petty producers': small artisans, freeholding peasants who produced, in whole or in part, for the market, and small manufacturing operations, or 'proto industries', chiefly in the wool districts of Flanders, Lombardy and Picardy.[16] These industrious artisans and small merchants – not yet capitalist and quite distinct from the wealthy merchant families that ruled cities like Genoa, Florence or Venice – became more numerous starting at the end of the eleventh century. They came to play a vital role in the growing crisis of feudalism that would reach its peak in the fourteenth century. They affirmed their independence in relation to feudal lords and improved their social status as their industriousness and commercial orientation was accepted or even, as Albertanus of Brescia argued, viewed as a pleasing virtue in the eyes of God. They relied on the commons to affirm their social position. This was true of the English rural gentry whose independence was based on the access to common land with their grazing rights and *estovers*. It was true of the urban artisans who relied on the common knowledge and social capital of the guilds. Indeed, the guilds created something like a market commons, offering the kinds of protection that enabled market participation and providing the legal and institutional framework necessary for the expansion of commerce and manufacture. These new organizations were fundamental for the formation of an infrastructure for a modern market economy. As virtually all contributions to the complicated 'transition debates' agree, the petty producers, both urban and rural, that relied on these new institutions for support and strength would play a vital role in undermining the feudal system, and prepare the way for the transition towards capitalism.[17]

Increasingly, these petty producers also supported and were mobilized by a vision of a more egalitarian commons-based market society, a society marked by what Marx would later call 'petty commodity exchange'. This vision of the market as an integral component of a new civil society founded on reciprocity, freedom and a new kind of secular individualism informed the economic thought of the Italian 'umanisti civili' of the twelfth to fourteenth centuries. It was supported by the guilds and new universities that acted as sources of legal and institutional innovation. These ideas would persist as a radical undercurrent throughout European history, to resurface in many forms. In the German peasant rebellions of the sixteenth century, they would inspire the formation of puritan movements. In the English revolution they guided the defence against growing enclosures on the part of movements like the Levellers and the Diggers, who would invoke, among other things, the Magna Carta as a bulwark against new forms of appropriation and exploitation. Drawing on this tradition, the puritans could unite the English middle class of petty producers in a fight against the corporations that had by now become conservative organizations supported by royal privilege. This tradition found a wider and more secular diffusion in the eighteenth century as the expansion of a print-based popular culture constituted a virtual 'political education of the common man'. At least on an ideological level this tradition kept inspiring those industrious entrepreneurs that later pioneered the industrial revolution and turned into capitalists facing an increasingly organized labour movement while, at least at face value, remaining faithful to the egalitarian roots of their often puritan religious convictions.[18]

For a long time the standard wisdom has been that the medieval commons acted as an obstacle to the development of markets and capitalism. However, there is something to be said also for the reverse scenario. The commons supported the transition to capitalism in at least three ways. First, they supported the emergence of a new 'middle class' of petty producers who relied on the commons to engage in market exchange. These petty producers became key actors in social movements challenging feudal privilege (in particular in the wake of the Black Death). Later they became the carrying strata of the 'protestant ethic' that made an important contribution to the development of capitalism in the West. Second, the commons were institutionalized in the form of guilds and fraternities who contributed to developing the basic institutions of an evolving market society. Third, the commons became a catalyst for social movements and an advancing 'civil society' that promoted 'modern' ideas of freedom and equality that, although often focused on addressing or criticizing market inequalities, did provide a decisive ideological support for the formation of such a 'capitalist spirit'. Overall, the commons supported a new industrious economy combining market exchange with a more modern social vision. This industrious economy provided an alternative for outcasts from the feudal systems, popular outcasts and 'masterless men' at first, but eventually also feudal seigneurs who gradually discovered that market activity could form a viable alternative to a feudal economy marked by declining productivity levels.

This story suggests that it is possible to trace the roots of an industrious modernity further back than the puritan revolution that Weber's narrative centres on. The point of doing so is not to engage in a mere history of ideas. Nor is the point to offer a critique of Weber – he is of course right in suggesting that it was the puritan movements that coalesced these ideas and acted as the 'switchman' that enabled them to have a greater impact on the European modernization process. Rather the point is to underline two important parallels. First, the feudal economy in the fourteenth century shows many similarities with industrial capitalism today. Like in the European fourteenth century, productivity levels today are stalling, in part because of ecological constraints and the population is growing. At the same time, levels of exploitation are increasing as the elites are ever more detached from the lives of ordinary people. The result is an exodus, to the cities in the Middle Ages, to alternative life projects today. Now, like then, ecological deterioration points towards a looming disaster, although perhaps not at the scale of the Black Death that killed off a third of the European population between 1347 and 1351, possibly the most significant destructive event in the history of the West. By that time traditional hierarchies and social structures had been partially undermined by the spread of market exchange – like they are undermined today by the spread of digital technologies and the social forms that they enable. In the wake of the Black Death this led to new large-scale and concentrated movements like the Grande Jacquerie in the aftermath of the French defeat at the Battle of Poitiers in 1356, or the English Peasants Revolt of 1381. In all of these events a new stratum of industrious market-oriented petty producers played a vital part.[19] Like the petty producers that are emerging around the potential of digital technologies today, they relied on the market as a means of subsistence and on the commons, rural or urban, as an important means of production. Like the industrious entrepreneurs of today, they embraced a vison where economic activity was also a way to change the world – to better one's situation, or to simply do good, 'to have an impact' we would say today. The point of this comparison is not to suggest that history is repeating itself and that we find ourselves in a new Middle Age, as Umberto Eco famously suggested in 1977. It is rather to suggest that we might have an alternative to the 'Great

Transformation' of the nineteenth century or the 'Great Revolutions' of the eighteenth as a model for how social change might come about. The transition from feudalism to capitalism was not a single event, it was not a *revolution*, but a complicated process where the carrier group of a new society emerged out of the ruins of an old, destroyed in effect by an ecological crisis.

The dynamic was similar to what we are witnessing today. Feudalism put in motion a process of social acceleration: an intensification of social and productive relations. This realized a new kind of commons that acted as the foundation for the emergence of new market-oriented relations of production. These new industrious relations of production grew more powerful and attractive as an alternative to a declining feudal system. And they became more difficult to contain within that order. In the fourteenth century a combined economic and ecological disaster effectively 'broke the backbone of the feudal order' and opened up the field for the affirmation of a new industrious market economy. Eventually this was joined by powerful elites, large merchants that shifted their basis of accumulation from trade to manufacture and production, and feudal lords who engaged in market exchange and commercial agriculture as an alternative to declining land rents. The 'spatial fix' provided by conquest and colonial expansion further changed the face of the medieval commons-based economy, making it less industrious and more industrial in shape. Indeed, starting in the seventeenth century we see growing conflicts between its new industrial capitalist part and its remaining industrious capital-poor part, a conflict that is largely settled in the eighteenth century by the elimination of the guilds and the privatization of the commons, and later by the defeat of culture and life forms of artisan workers. Despite the disappearance of its real basis, this industrious economy remains as an ideological ideal to inspire the classical liberalism that guided the transition to industrial modernity in the eighteenth and nineteenth centuries. Like then, industrious entrepreneurs aiming to change the world, while perhaps not knowing into what exactly, might be what fills up the void left by an industrial capitalism in decline.[20]

Imagining a transition

The Black Death broke the backbone of feudal society. What ensued was a period of popular empowerment: wages rose as labour became scarce and social control broke down in the countryside. The feudal response was to step up repression, to constrain the rising costs of labour and to engage in new waves of land reclamations. In some cases, this was successful, but it also spurred a new cycle of movements, more coordinated, centralized and intense. At the same time the productive power of the industrious economy increased as guilds were instrumental in developing new kinds of capital-intensive productive techniques that could compensate for the lack of workers, and that contributed significantly to the development of manufacturing. Indeed, to some extent the ensuing Renaissance might also be a result of the inability to contain bottom-up innovation as the relative power of workers increased and repressive state power was hollowed out. New relations of production emerged out of the ruins of the feudal order, building on institutions and mechanisms that were already in place, but that had remained repressed. Eventually the remaining feudal elites were forced to accept the new situation and join the ranks of the rising merchant class.

The main way in which an emerging market society was contained within the control of established elites was through the intensification of the scope, if not the actual power of the state. The formation of the absolutist state entailed, among other things, a pioneering number of new techniques of governance, like statistics or 'political arithmetic' and the new disciplines like political economy and demographics. (Indeed, Michel Foucault locates the origins of modern disciplinary power to the new techniques of confinement and population control that developed in response to the repeated outbreaks of the plague that marked the fourteenth to seventeenth centuries.) The absolutist state resulted from a compromise between the nobility, large merchants and some of the guilds and organized around strengthened royal power and an expanded state bureaucracy, which partly absorbed the old nobility, as in the case of the French *noblesse de robe*. It was a response both to new, more radicalized forms of popular unrest, and to an intensified bottom-up market activity, to an accelerating industrious 'revolution' that it sought to contain. However, as economic growth accelerated in the eighteenth century, the conservative nature of this ancien régime became increasingly evident and its heavy-handed regulations came to clash with the advance of market society ever more frequently.

In early modern Europe the preservation of elite power and the relatively continuous nature of the transition between feudalism and the new capitalist order that began to take shape rested on the ability to export the contradictions that had driven the collapse of feudalism, through a globalization of the capitalist economy. Colonial expansion and the plantation economy could compensate for the Malthusian problem of limited agricultural productivity, absorb the surplus population that resulted from enclosures and land reclamations and provide an extended base for the 'original accumulation' of capital necessary to support the expansion of manufacture and later industry. Today such a spatial fix is no longer available. Capitalism has already been completely globalized and its very essence, the drive towards continuous growth, is running into ecological limits. Again, this is not an absolute obstacle: the colonization of other planets might be an option in the future, and an intensification of capitalist accumulation based on the commoditization of regenerative ecological practices might also be a possibility. But we are far from there yet in terms of technological and, above all, social and institutional development. What sort of alternative might the industrious economy provide?

At the heart of the social and economic imaginary of contemporary industrious modernity there is a call for decentralization. Peer-production projects, blockchain-based economic circuits and new guild-like institutions all point towards an economy governed by local interests or direct user participation, with little in terms of centralized control. Such claims for decentralization are not entirely new. Instead, the movement between centralized and decentralized relations of production appears to be a constant feature of capitalist development. In the nineteenth century, industrial districts made up of small-scale, flexible and highly skilled units remained competitive for a long time, in particular in sectors less prone to standardization like machine tools and luxury textiles. Indeed, the Jacquard loom can be understood as an early numerical technology for enhancing such flexible specialization. Such small-scale 'guild or yeoman industrialization', rested on collaboration between producers with relatively equal market power, communitarian governance, and it implied small differences between capital and labour. Its virtual elimination in favour of large-scale mass production in the post-war period was less a matter of technological possibility and more a question of political will. Indeed, such flexible specialization soon resurfaced in the industrial districts of Northern and Central Italy as a response to the break-up of the Fordist hegemony. It appears that phases of decentralization build on the availability of new commons, the common skills 'in the air' or Alfred Marshall's industrial districts in the nineteenth century, the digital commons that drive today's industriousness. Subsequent phases of centralization build on the appropriation of such commons, as in the case of the platform-based corporate supply chains that began to take over from local community participation in governing industrial districts as globalization set in in earnest in the mid-1990s, or the advance of platform capitalism today.[21]

Is it possible to resist such pressures for centralization? This would depend on the strength of these forces, but it would also depend on the ability of the actors in a decentralized economic system to acquire and wield state power in some form. With the present political system, it seems very difficult to imagine a decentralized state, built on a diversity of local interests and value horizons, like the plurality of communities pioneered by more radical champions of commonism, without the system succumbing to the centrifugal forces of local interest. However, new political technologies like blockchain-based tokenization systems promise to automate the execution of legal guarantees and thus render political institutions immune to such local takeovers. If currencies, taxation and markets are governed automatically, according to inalienable principles inscribed in their codes, then once such principles have been established, they remain immune to pressure from local and particular interests. Will the potential of blockchains, or some similar, perhaps more efficient and less energy-consuming system to decentralize everything, become the political infrastructure of a new industrious economy?

For now, the required institutional innovations exist only as more or less science fiction-like 'white papers' (the ubiquitous visionary documents that accompany blockchain ventures). There does, however, seem to be a cultural shift under way. Indeed, the term industrious 'modernity' seeks to capture the somewhat elusive nature of this phenomenon. What we are talking about is not a movement, not a class (at least not yet), but a common experience and an emerging common imaginary.

The transition from feudalism to capitalism in Europe was a drawn-out and complicated affair, and a very violent one. Weber's contribution was to point out the crucial role of a new imaginary – what he calls the protestant ethic. While many other factors explain the 'Great Divergence' that the development of European capitalism created, the existence of such a new imaginary remains a necessary, if not sufficient, cause. As I have suggested in this chapter, the protestants and their 'ethic' were the outcome of a longer story of the development of industrious relations of production and an accompanying mentality – a story that goes back at least to the turn of the second millennium. However, it was only once this emerging mentality could coalesce into a coherent imaginary, with its own vision of modernity, that it was able to act as a 'switchman' to guide European (and, with time, increasingly also other) masses to modernity. Today, we remain locked into the capitalist realism like the ancien régime remained locked into the ideals and worldviews of its feudal past. However, we might sense the seeds of a different imaginary emerging from contemporary commons-based industrious actors. We seem to be witnessing a return of a pre-industrial conception of value, building on a combination of authenticity and reputation as a criterion of value. (Just like guilds operated with a conception of value combining the notion of intrinsic quality with the reputation of master craftsmen.) This is most visible in the food economy where a new wave of neo-rural farmers is emerging worldwide, driving a 'quality' revolution based on a combination of the rediscovery of traditional production methods, digital technology commons and an orientation to ecological diversity and sustainability. However, a similar vision seems to be guiding the whole new industrious universes, from 'Southern' peasant struggles, like the *Via Campesina* movement, via hipster farmers to new blockchain-enabled economic communities. All are oriented around a quest for 'value sovereignty', the ability to, like the medieval guilds, engage in market participation while safeguarding the highly particular ethos that orients the specific practice that they engage in. Just as the experience of the Black Death served to intensify the sense of pious intensity that eventually developed into puritanism, and to delegitimize the established church, so the experience of going deeper into the Anthropocene might very well intensify the power and attraction of this new imaginary, enabling it, along the way, to develop its own political institutions.

Notes

Chapter 1: To Change the World: On Industrious Modernity

1 The quote appears in various versions in Gramsci's *Prison Notebooks*, along with the sensation, which many of us share today, that the 'Old is dying, but the new cannot yet be born'; see Antonio Gramsci, *Selections from the Prison Notebooks* (eds. Quintin Hoare and Geoffrey Nowell Smith), New York: International Publishers, 1971. The term 'Changemakers' was introduced and trademarked by the Ashoka Foundation in 2010, see https://trademarks.justia.com/779/24/changemakers-77924088.html and https://www.changemakers.com/. On Changemakers as an identity, see Carolina Bandinelli and Adam Arvidsson, 'Brand yourself a ChangeMaker', *Journal of Macromarketing*, 33(1), 2013, 67–71.

2 Marshall Berman, *All that is Solid Melts into Air: The Experience of Modernity*, New York: Simon & Schuster, 1982, p. 15. Modernity is admittedly a vague term. Berman uses it to designate a particular mode of experiencing the world. I use it as a 'sensitizing concept' – a tool to think with that does not so much designate or refer to a precisely defined 'thing' as much as it opens up a point of view. On how the future lost its directions, see Arjun Appadurai, *The Future as Cultural Fact: Essays on the Global Condition*, London: Verso, 2013; and, earlier, Ulrich Beck, *Risk Society: Towards a New Modernity?* London: Sage, 1992.

3 Mark Fisher, *Capitalist Realism: Is There No Alternative?* London: Zero Books, 2009.

4 Although he stays away from explicit 'value judgements', the last part of the essay on *The Protestant Ethic* suggests that Weber did not think that the Protestants would have liked it in the iron cage of industrial modernity that they contributed to build; see Max Weber, *The Protestant Ethic and the Spirit of Modern Capitalism*, Oxford: Oxford University Press, 2011 [1904–5]. On the many-headed hydra, see Marcus Rediker and Peter Linebaugh, *Many-Headed Hydra: The Hidden History of the Revolutionary Atlantic*, Boston, MA: Beacon Press, 2000. The origins of notions of civil society in the 'commercial revolution' of medieval Europe will be discussed in further detail in chapter 5.

5 See David Graeber, *Bullshit Jobs: A Theory*, New York: Simon and Schuster, 2018. On the puritan sects as an answer to precarity, see Michael Waltzer, *The Revolution of the Saints*, Cambridge, MA: Harvard University Press, 1965, pp. 308–16.

6 Fernand Braudel, *Civilization and Capitalism, 15th–18th Century. Vol III. The Perspective of the World*, New York: Harper & Row, 1984, p. 630.

7 For examples of such neo-apocalyptic social thought, see Anna Lowenhaupt Tsing, *The Mushroom at the End of the World: On the Possibility of Life in Capitalist Ruins*, Princeton, NJ: Princeton University Press, 2015; and Donna Haraway, *Staying with the Trouble: Making Kin in the Chthulucene*, Duham, NC: Duke University Press, 2016.

8 Fisher, *Capitalist Realism*, p. 3.

9 Pankaj Mishra, *The Age of Anger*, London: Penguin, 2017. On depression and soaring rates of drug addiction in the UK, see Nicola Slawson, 'Young Britons have never been unhappier', *The Guardian*, 5 April 2018, https://www.theguardian.com/society/2018/apr/05/young-people-have-never-been-unhappier-research-suggests (accessed 8 May 2018).

10 According to the Global Entrepreneurship Monitor, the rate of 'early stage entrepreneurial activity' (i.e., having started a business in the last three years) ranges from 16.8 per cent in 'factor-driven economies' (i.e., what used to be known as 'developing economies') to 9.1 per cent in 'innovation-driven' (i.e., 'developed') economies. Depending on the contexts, between one-tenth and one-eighth of the people aged 18–64 are engaged in early-stage entrepreneurial activity. Between 58 and 67 per cent perceive entrepreneurship to be a 'good career choice'; see Global Entrepreneurship Monitor 2016–17, pp. 18–22, available at https://www.gemconsortium.org/report (accessed 8 May 2018). On action, see Hannah Arendt, *The Human Condition*, Chicago, IL: University of Chicago Press, 1958. On

'ontological security', see Anthony Giddens, *Modernity and Self-Identity*, Stanford, CA: Stanford University Press.

11 Paul Mason, *Postcapitalism: A Guide to our Future*, London: Macmillan, 2016; Jeremy Rifkin, *The Zero Marginal Cost Society: The Internet of Things, the Collaborative Commons, and the Eclipse of Capitalism*, London: St. Martin's Press, 2014.

Chapter 2: The Crisis of Digital Capitalism

1 For the quote form Robert Solow, articulating what was known as the 'productivity paradox', see Robert Solow, 'We'd better watch out', *The New York Times Book Review*, 12 July 1987. On the spread of digital media and its consequences for everyday sociality, see Sherry Turkle, *Alone Together: Why We Expect More from Technology and Less from Each Other*, New York: Basic Books, 2012. On early visions of the new 'frictionless' digital economy, see, for example, Nicholas Negroponte, *Being Digital*, New York: Knopf, 1999; or Bill Gates, *The Road Ahead*, London: Penguin, 1996. For an academic discussion of these early utopian visions, see Jens Schroter, 'The internet and "frictionless capitalism"', *TripleC*, 10(2), 2012, 302–12.

2 On the reduction in extreme poverty, see 'Towards the end of poverty' (editorial), *The Economist*, 1 June 2013. On the important role of China in this process, see Giovanni Arrighi, 'The winding paths of capital' (interview by David Harvey), *The New Left Review*, 56, March–April 2009, 78ff. On the increase in inequality, see Thomas Picketty, *Capital in the 21st Century*, Cambridge, MA: Harvard University Press, 2014; on 'iSlavery' and growing inequality in China, see Jack Qiu, *Goodbye iSlave*, Chicago, IL: University of Illinois Press, 2016; on decreasing prospects for middle-class knowledge workers, see Michael Hobbes, 'Millenials are screwed', *Huffington Post*, (no date), http://highline.huffingtonpost.com/articles/en/poor-millennials/ (accessed 18 April 2018). On the contemporary precariat, see Guy Standing, *The Precariat: The New Dangerous Class*, London: Bloomsbury Academic, 2011; for a global context, Ben Scully, 'Precarity North and South: a Southern critique of Guy Standing', *Global Labour Journal*, 7(2), 2016, 160–73; Craig Jeffrey, *Timepass: Youth, Class and the Politics of Waiting in India*, Stanford, CA: Stanford University Press, 2010; Mike Davis, *Planet of Slums*, London: Verso, 2006.

3 Naomi Klein, *This Changes Everything. Capitalism vs. The Climate*, New York: Simon & Schuster, 2014.

4 The phrase about it being easier to imagine the end of the world than the demise of capitalism is usually attributed to Marxist critic Frederic Jameson; see Fisher, *Capitalist Realism*, pp. 21–30.

5 Joel Mokyr, 'Entrepreneurship and the Industrial Revolution in Britain', in David Landes, Joel Mokyr and William Baumol (eds.), *The Invention of Enterprise: Entrepreneurship from Ancient Mesopotamia to Modern Times*, Princeton, NJ: Princeton University Press, 2010, pp. 183–210.

6 See Eva Illouz (ed.), *Emotions as Commodities: Capitalism, Consumption and Authenticity*, London: Routledge, 2017.

7 Peter Thiel, 'Competition is for losers', *The Wall Street Journal*, 12 September 2014, https://www.wsj.com/articles/peter-thiel-competition-is-for-losers-1410535536 (accessed 7 September 2017).

8 See Fernand Braudel, *Civilization and Capitalism, 15th to 18th Century (vols I–III)*, London: Collins, 1981–4. As one of Braudel's most illustrious followers, Giovanni Arrighi put it: 'The capitalist character of market-based development is not determined by the presence of capitalist institutions and dispositions but by the relation of state power to capital. Add as many capitalists as you like to a market economy, but unless the state has been subordinated to their class interest, the market economy remains non-capitalist', Giovanni Arrighi, *Adam Smith in Beijing: Lineages of the Twenty-First Century*, London: Verso, 2007, pp. 331–2.

9 For an overview of the history of capitalism, see Christopher A. Bayly, *The Birth of the Modern World, 1780–1914*, Oxford, Blackwell, 2003; on industrialization as a 'disruptive' transformation, see Karl Polanyi, *The Great Transformation: The Political and Economic Origins of our Time*, Boston, MA: Beacon Press, 1957.

10 Marx's theory of capitalism as a 'metabolic rift' derives from his critique of Malthus; see John Bellamy Foster, 'Marx's theory of metabolic rift: classical foundations for environmental sociology', *American Journal of Sociology*, 105(2), 1999, 366–405. It has been developed in the recent work of environmental sociologists; see Jason W. Moore, *Capitalism in the Web of Life: Ecology and the Accumulation of Capital*, London: Verso Books, 2015; Raj Patel and Jason W. Moore, *History of the World in Seven Cheap Things: A Guide to Capitalism, Nature and the Future of the Planet*, Berkeley, CA: University of California Press, 2017. For the concept of 'bio-capitalism', see Andrea Fumagalli, 'Twenty theses on contemporary capitalism (cognitive biocapitalism)', *Angelaki*, 16(3), 2011, 7–17.

11 Marx devotes several pages in *Capital, vol. I* to the difficulties encountered by early industrialists when dealing with former peasants newly arrived in the factories. The theme has also been dear to early scholars in the English Cultural Studies tradition and the historians inspired by them. See Edward P. Thompson, 'Time, work-discipline, and industrial capitalism', *Past & Present*, 38, 1967, 56–97. Max Weber framed the issue as that of acquiring a modern economic rationality. He wrote of the (ideal-typical) pre-industrial worker: 'The opportunity of earning less appealed to him less than the idea of working less. He did not ask: "If I produce as much as possible, how much money will I earn today?" Rather he formulated the question differently: "How long must I work in order to earn the amount of money – 2½ marks – I have earned until now and that has fulfilled my *traditional* economic needs?"', Max Weber, *The Protestant Ethic*, p. 85 (italics in original).

12 On the creation of an orderly and predictable population as a core component of the Western modernization project, see Marshall Berman, *All that is Solid Melts into Air*. Classic references here are Norbert Elias, *The Civilizing Process*, Oxford: Blackwell, 1978; and Michel Foucault, *Surveiller et punir: Naissance de la prison*, Paris: Gallimard, 1975. On the role of consumer culture in this process, see Gary Cross, *Time and Money: The Making of Consumer Culture*, London: Routledge, 1993.

13 On the history of the human, and in particular capitalist, impact on the planetary ecology, see Christophe Bonneuil and Jean-Baptiste Fressoz, *The Shock of the Anthropocene*, London: Verso, 2017. Patel and Moore (*History of the World*) give a detailed history of capitalism as based on the creation of a number of artificially cheap things, among them energy and labour. On the role of fossil fuels in the 'Great Divergence' that set off industrializing Britain (and subsequently the West) from the rest, see Kenneth Pomeranz, *The Great Divergence: China, Europe, and the Making of the Modern World Economy*, Princeton, NJ: Princeton University Press, 2000.

14 Many scholars have offered descriptions of 'industrial', 'high', 'Fordist' or 'organized' modernity. Among the best are David Harvey, *The Condition of Postmodernity*, Oxford: Blackwell, 1990, and Michel Aglietta, *A Theory of Capitalist Regulation*, London: Verso, 1978. An ideal type is a concept developed by Max Weber. As a methodological tool, an 'ideal type' consists in an abstraction of social reality into a generic concept that, while it does not actually represent any empirically existing reality, helps us understand and speak about such reality. An

ideal type can be understood as a sort of conceptual map that allows us to navigate the empirical terrain. It should not be taken as a truthful description of that terrain.

15 On the argument that capitalist growth has stalled because of the exhaustion of necessary space for expansion, see Patel and Moore, *History of the World*, pp. 18–21. On the suggestion that Adam Smith could not envision the radical transformation that came with the industrial revolution but had something much more modest in mind, see Deirdre N. McCloskey, *Bourgeois Dignity: Why Economics Can't Explain the Modern World*, Chicago, IL: University of Chicago Press, 2010, p. 34.

16 On the decline in manufacturing profitability during the 1970s, see Robert Brenner, 'New boom or new bubble?', *New Left Review*, 25, January–February 2004, 57–8; 'The Economics of Global Turbulence: A Special Report on the World Economy', *New Left Review*, 229, May–June 1998, 93.

17 On the connection between digital technologies and the counterculture of the 1970s, see Fred Turner, *From Counterculture to Cyberculture: Stewart Brand, the Whole Earth Network, and the Rise of Digital Utopianism*, Chicago, IL: University of Chicago Press, 2010.

18 On industrial restructuring as a response to worker resistance, see Adam Arvidsson and Nicolai Peitersen, *The Ethical Economy: Rebuilding Value after the Crisis*, New York: Columbia University Press, 2013; the classic reference is Mario Tronti, *Workers and Capital*, London: Verso, 2019.

19 On capital concentration in global supply chains, see Bennet Harrison, *Lean and Mean: The Changing Landscape of Corporate Power in the Age of Flexibility*, New York: Basic Books, 1994; John Bellamy Foster, 'Monopoly and competition in twenty-first century capitalism', *Monthly Review*, 62(11), 2011, 1–43. On the role of intangible assets in explaining productivity differentials, see Michael Roberts, 'Capitalism without capital – or capital without capitalism', https://thenextrecession. wordpress.com/2017/12/10/capitalism-without-capital-or-capital-without-capitalism/ (accessed 18 April 2018).

20 On the new forms of financialization that have developed in the last decades, see Randy Martin, *The Financialization of Everyday Life*, Philadelphia, PA: Temple University Press, 2002; Dick Bryan and Michael Rafferty, *Capitalism with Derivatives: A Political Economy of Financial Derivatives, Capital and Class*, New York: Springer, 2005.

21 On the role of financial power in contemporary capitalism, and on the rise in financial rent as a component of corporate earnings, see Andrea Fumagalli, 'Twenty theses on contemporary

capitalism'. For a detailed empirical analysis, see Gérard Duménil and Dominique Lévy, 'The real and financial components of corporate profitability (USA 1948–2000)', Working Paper, CEPREMAP-ENS, Paris, 2005, http://citeseerx.ist.psu. edu/viewdoc/download?doi=10.1.1.572.8956&rep=rep1&typ e=pdf (accessed 10 March 2019).

22 On the decline in research profitability in the US, see Nicholas Bloom, Charles Jones, John van Reenen and Michael Webb, 'Are ideas getting harder to find?', National Bureau of Economic Research Working Paper No. 23782, 2017, http://www.nber. org/papers/w23782 (accessed 18 April 2018). For a more general argument, see Robert J. Gordon, *The Rise and Fall of American Growth: The US Standard of Living since the Civil War*, Princeton, NJ: Princeton University Press, 2017.

23 On the over-accumulation of capital and its consequences, see Javier Espinoza, 'Private equity: flood of cash triggers buyout bubble fears', *Financial Times*, 23 January 2018, https://www.ft.com/content/3d13da34-f6bb-11e7-8715-e94187b3017e (accessed 19 April 2018); Arash Massoudi, James Fontanella-Khan and Don Weinland, 'Global M&A exceeds $3tn for fourth straight year', *Financial Times*, 28 December 2017, https://www.ft.com/content/9f0270aa-eabf-11e7-bd17-521324c81e23 (accessed 19 April 2018). On Apple's cash reserves, see Lauren Feiner, 'Apple now has $237.1 billion in cash on hand', *CNBC*, 1 November 2018, https://www.cnbc.com/2018/11/01/apple-now-has-237point1-billion-in-cash-on-hand.html (accessed 10 January 2019).

24 As Henry Heller writes of this period: 'by the seventeenth century the Italian economy was reduced to local economies exploiting an immediate hinterland through rents and taxes', a state that would persist more or less until industrialization took off in the late nineteenth century; see Henry Heller, *The Birth of Capitalism*, London: Pluto Press, 2011, p. 59.

25 On Machiavelli in the context of the decline of the 'Italian world economy', see Luigino Bruni and Stefano Zamagni, *Economia Civile: Efficienza, Equità, Felicità Pubblica*, Bologna: il Mulino, 2004, pp. 62ff. On re-feudalization as a symptom of the end of each historical cycle of capitalist accumulation, see Giovanni Arrighi, *The Long Twentieth Century*, London: Verso, 1994, pp. 96–109.

26 On the quest for alternatives to factory work among African workers, see Bill Freund, *The African Worker*, Cambridge: Cambridge University Press, 1988; for China, Shaohua Zhan and Lingli Huang, 'Rural roots of current migrant labor shortage in China: development and labor empowerment

in a situation of incomplete proletarization', *Studies in Comparative International Development*, 48(1), 2012, 81–111; cf. Scully, 'Precarity North and South'.

27 The disappearance of 'good jobs' has been a standard theme of Critical Labour studies since the1970s; see Andre Gorz, *Farewell to the Working Class: An Essay on Post-Industrial Socialism*, London: Pluto Press, 1997. Many of the 'good jobs' have been replaced by lower paid, more insecure or precarious occupations in the service industries – the so-called 'Walmart economy'; see Vanessa Parlette and Deborah Cowen, 'Dead malls: suburban activism, local spaces, global logistics', *International Journal of Urban and Regional Research*, 35(4), 2011, 794–811. Present trends towards automation, digitalization or 'platformization' is threatening these very 'Walmart jobs' as the profitability of large retailing operations (among them Walmart) is undermined by the expansion of e-commerce and, above all, Amazon. com; see Scheherazade Daneshkhu, 'Consumer goods: big brands battle with the "little guys"', *Financial Times*, 28 February 2018, https://www.ft.com/content/4aa58b22-1a81-11e8-aaca-4574d7dabfb6 (accessed 19 April 2018).

Chapter 3: The Industrious Economy

1 On the curves spiking as a result of the industrial take-off, see Bonneuil and Fressoz, *The Shock of the Anthropocene*, pp. 10–11. On the 'disruptive' effects of the industrial revolution, see Karl Polanyi, *The Great Transformation: The Political and Economic Origins of Our Time*, New York: Farrar & Rinehart, 1944; on industrial modernity's reliance on large-scale projects, see Harvey, *The Condition of Postmodernity*; on its disregard for nature and 'people without history', Eric Wolf, *Europe and the People without History*, Berkeley, CA: University of California Press, 1982.

2 Adam Smith, *An Inquiry into the Wealth of Nations*, New York: Random House, 2003 [1776], pp. 23–4. On Adam Smith's conception of the economy as morally grounded, see Emma Rothschild, *Economic Sentiments: Adam Smith, Concordet and the Enlightenment*, Cambridge, MA: Harvard University Press, 2013. On the modern 'disembedding' of the economy, see Polanyi, *The Great Transformation*.

3 Fernand Braudel, *Afterthoughts on Material Civilization and Capitalism*, Baltimore, MD: Johns Hopkins University Press, 1977; on advanced pre-capitalist economies as industrious, marked by high-level Smithian equilibrium, see, for example,

Andre Gunder-Frank, *ReOrient*, Berkeley, CA: University of
California Press, 1998; for China in particular, Ho-Fung Hung,
'Imperial China and capitalist Europe in the 18th century global
economy', *Review (Fernand Braudel Center)*, 24(4), 2001,
473–513.

4 See Arrighi, *Adam Smith in Beijing*, pp. 40ff.

5 The most famous denunciation of the 'Asiatic mode of
  production' remains Karl Wittvogel's *Oriental Despotism: A
  Study of Total Power*, New Haven, CT: Yale University Press,
  1957. The concept of an 'Asiatic mode of production' was
  subsequently rehabilitated by Soviet economic historians in
  the post-war years; see Stephen Dunn, *The Fall and Rise of
  the Asiatic Mode of Production*, London: Routledge, 1982.
  On resistance to bazaar economies, street vending and other
  manifestations of 'traditional' industriousness in the context
  of colonial and post-colonial projects of modernization, see
  Jonathan Shapiro Anjaria, *The Slow Boil: Street Food, Rights
  and Public Space in Mumbai*, Stanford, CA: Stanford University
  Press, 2016.

6 From 1980 to 2015 the share of the US workforce employed
  in small companies (less than 100 employees) has been reduced
  from 40 to 34 per cent. At the same time the share of
  the workforce employed in big companies (more than 5,000
  employees) has increased from 30 to 34 per cent; see Ben
  Casselman, 'A start-up slump is a drag on the economy. Big
  business may be to blame', *The New York Times*, 20 September
  2017, https://www.nytimes.com/2017/09/20/business/economy/
  startup-business.html (accessed 10 January 2019). The rise of
  entrepreneurship is most significant in two sectors: knowledge/
  work and 'popular entrepreneurship' among the 'global poor'.
  UK data show that 89 per cent of the significant rise in the
  number of business establishments that has taken place from
  2000 (59 per cent) is accounted for by self-employing businesses;
  see Federation of Small Businesses, UK Small Business Statistics,
  https://www.fsb.org.uk/media-centre/small-business-statistics
  (accessed 16 November 2017). The Italian economy has seen a
  rise in the percentage of self-employed from 48.1 per cent of all
  businesses in 1981, to 58.6 per cent in 2001. As a share of the
  workforce, the self-employed have increased from 10.5 to 15.2
  per cent in the same period; see Istat, Serie Storiche, Industria,
  http://seriestoriche.istat.it/index.php?id=1&no_cache=1&tx_
  usercento_centofe%5Bcategoria%5D=14&tx_usercento_
  centofe%5Baction%5D=show&tx_usercento_centofe%5Bco
  ntroller%5D=Categoria&cHash=b92882f45d2a3f833d3997
  2669d7bef3 (accessed 16 November 2017). In the digital

economy, the number of start-ups and similar 'innovative' ventures has equally grown. Although the share of new entrepreneurs in the US who have a college degree roughly mirrors the share of graduates in the population as a whole (around 30 per cent), this figure is the result of a 30 per cent rise in the share of new entrepreneurs who also possess a degree since 1996. This suggests that college graduates, who used to be less inclined to start a business than the population in general, have come to increasingly choose this route. See *2017 Kauffman Index of Startup Activity*, Ewing Marion Kauffman Foundation, 2017, p. 16. Entrepreneurship is most prevalent among the 'global poor', young people (in particular), in what are euphemistically referred to as 'factor-driven' economies, and migrants. Such popular entrepreneurship makes up the lion's share of the global growth in entrepreneurship levels. The 2017 *Global Entrepreneurship Report* shows that 'total early-stage entrepreneurial activity' (summarizing the percentage of the population engaged in new business creation, those owning a small business that has been active for more than 3 months but less than 42 months, and employee entrepreneurial activity (that is, employees generating new business for their employers) is highest in 'factor-driven economies' (29.2 per cent of the population) and lowest in 'innovation-driven economies' (20.9 per cent); see Global Entrepreneurship Research Association, *Global Entrepreneurship Report*, 2017, p. 21, http://www.gemconsortium.org/report (accessed 17 November 2017). For an overview of the persistence of small-scale industrious businesses even in advanced industrial economies, see Alfonso Morales, 'Peddling policy: street vending in historical and contemporary context', *International Journal of Sociology and Social Policy*, 20(3/4), 2000, 76–98; Alejandro Portes and Saskia Sassen-Koob, 'Making it underground: comparative material on the informal sector in Western market economies', *American Journal of Sociology*, 93(1), 1987, 30–61.

7 On the structure and conflicts of Shenzhen's electronics industry, see Qiu, *Goodbye iSlave*; Joonkoo Lee, Jong-Cheol Kim and Jinho Lim, 'Globalization and divergent paths of industrial development: mobile phone manufacturing in China, Japan, South Korea and Taiwan', *Journal of Contemporary Asia*, 46(2), 2016, 222–46; Mary-Ann O'Donnell, Winnie Wong and Jonathan Bach (eds.), *Learning from Shenzhen: China's Post-Mao Experiment from Special Zone to Model City*, Chicago, IL: University of Chicago Press, 2017. On the 'modernization' and digitalization of Delhi's bazaars, see Ravi Sundaram, *Pirate Modernity: Delhi's Media Urbanism*, London:

Routledge, 2009; Maitrayee Deka, 'Embodied commons: knowledge and sharing in Delhi's electronic bazaars', *The Sociological Review*, 66(2), 2018, 365–80. On the 'new generation' of street vendors in Bangkok, see Chuthatip Maneepong and John Christopher Walsh, 'A new generation of Bangkok Street vendors: economic crisis as opportunity and threat', *Cities*, 34, 2013, 37–43.

8 On the street, or 'pirate' economy of poor-to-poor, see Alain Tarrius, *Etrangers de Passage: Poor to Poor, Peer to Peer*, La Tour d'Aigues: Editions de l'Aube, 2015; Gordon Mathews, Gustavo Lins Ribeiro and Carlos Alba Vega, *Globalization from Below: The World's Other Economy*, London: Routledge, 2012.

9 See Robert L. Afutu-Kotey, 'Young entrepreneurs in the mobile telephony sector in Ghana', in Katherine V. Gough and Thilde Langevang (eds.), *Young Entrepreneurs in Sub-Saharan Africa*, London: Routledge, 2016, pp. 167–80; Sebastiana Etzo and Guy Collender, 'The mobile phone "revolution" in Africa: rhetoric or reality?', *African Affairs*, 109(437), 2010, 659–68. On the use of free software, YouTube tutorials and other aspects of the digital commons among Bazaar 'tinkerers', see Maitrayee Deka, 'Street level tinkering in the times of "Make in India"', *Ephemera: Theory and Politics in Organization*, 17(4), 2017, 801–17.

10 Joseph Bernstein, 'How to make millions of hoverboards (almost) overnight', *Buzzfeed*, 27 November 2015, https://www.buzzfeed.com/josephbernstein/how-to-make-millions-of-hoverboards-almost-overnight?utm_term=.pvxYvDLaEj#.wb98XykRvr (accessed 8 May 2018).

11 For information on the overall size and market share of the Shanzhai system, see Michael Keane and Elaine Jing Zhao, 'Renegades on the frontier of innovation: the *Shanzhai* grassroots communities of Shenzhen in China's creative economy', *Euro-Asian Geography and Economics*, 53(2), 2012, 216–30. The link between Shanzhai cell phones and the movements of the 'Arab Spring' is suggested by Greg Lindsay, 'China's cell phone pirates are bringing down Middle Eastern governments', *FastCompany*, 11 June 2011.

12 Silvia Lindtner, Anna Greenspan and David Li, 'Designed in Shenzhen: Shanzhai manufacturing and maker entrepreneurs', *5th Decennial Aarhus Conference on Critical Alternatives*, 17 August 2015, p. 4. On the overall organization of the Shanzhai system, see Sheng Zhu and Yongjiang Shi, 'Shanzhai manufacturing: an alternative innovation phenomenon in China', *Journal of Science and Technology Policy in China*, 1(1), 2010,

29–49; Bai Gao, 'The informal economy in the era of information revolution and globalization: the Shanzhai cell phone industry in China', *Chinese Journal of Sociology*, 31(2), 2011, 1–41.

13 While 'very little is known' on the global counterfeit trade, a review of the available literature indicates that it has 'risen dramatically in recent years' and seen significant enhancement of 'technological and production capabilities'; see Thorstein Staake, Frédéric Thiesse and Elgar Fleisch, 'The emergence of counterfeit trade: a literature review', *European Journal of Marketing*, 43(3/4), 2009, 323, 325. On popular desires for branded (if counterfeited) goods, see Constantine Nakassis, 'Counterfeiting what? Aesthetics of brandedness and brand in Tamil Nadu, India', *Anthropological Quarterly*, 85(3), 2012, 701–21. For an overview of the literature on immigrant entrepreneurship, see Jan Rath and Robert Kloosterman, 'Outsiders' business: a critical review of research on immigrant entrepreneurship', *The International Migration Review*, 34(3), 2000, 657–81.

14 Maija Palmer, 'Cloud computing cuts start-up costs', *Financial Times*, 29 February 2012, https://www.ft.com/content/fc871bca-58e1-11e1-b9c6-00144feabdc0 (accessed 8 May 2018); see also *The Economist*, 'Why start-ups are leaving Silicon Valley', editorial, 30 August 2018, https://www.economist.com/leaders/2018/08/30/why-startups-are-leaving-silicon-valley (accessed 10 January 2019).

15 On US data for graduate entrepreneurship, see *2017 Kauffman Index of Start-up Activity*, p. 16. On China, Qunlian Hong, 'The major difficulties and countermeasures of current university graduates' entrepreneurship in China', *Journal of Chinese Entrepreneurship*, 3(3), 2011, 228–39. For a collection of anecdotes on young Chinese entrepreneurs in the knowledge economy, see Edward Tse, *China's Disruptors: How Alibaba, Xiaomi, Tencent, and Other Companies are Changing the Rules of Business*, London: Penguin, 2015. For a review of the literature on graduate entrepreneurship in BRIC countries, including data on motivations, see Ooi Yeng Keat, Christopher Selvarajah and Denny Meyer, 'Inclination towards entrepreneurship among university students: an empirical study of Malaysian university students', *International Journal of Business and Social Science*, 2(4), 2011, 206–20.

16 On social enterprise, see Carolina Bandinelli, *Social Enterprise and Neoliberalism: Making Money while Doing Good?* London: Rowman and Littlefield, forthcoming; Marshall Ganz, Tamara Kay and Jason Spicer, 'Social enterprise is not social change',

Stanford Social Innovation Review, Spring, 2018, https://ssir.org/articles/entry/social_enterprise_is_not_social_change (accessed 8 May 2018).

17 For a fairly comprehensive catalogue of commons-based peer-production initiatives, see the P2PFoundation Wiki, https://wiki.p2pfoundation.net/Main_Page; for theoretical accounts, Yochai Benkler, *The Wealth of Networks*, New Haven, CT: Yale University Press, 2006; Christopher Kelty, *Two Bits: The Cultural Significance of Free Software*, Durham, NC: Duke University Press, 2008; E. Gabriella Coleman, *Coding Freedom: The Ethics and Aesthetics of Hacking*, Princeton, NJ: Princeton University Press, 2012; Alessandro Delfanti, *Biohackers: The Politics of Open Science*, London: Pluto Press, 2013.

18 On African start-ups, see William Wallis, 'Smart Africa: Smartphones pave way for huge opportunities', *Financial Times*, 26 January 2016, https://www.ft.com/content/aba818a6-c392-11e5-808f-8231cd71622e (accessed 13 December 2017); David Pilling, 'Kenyans start to roam the silicon savannah', *Financial Times*, 27 April 2016, https://www.ft.com/content/1cda231c-0bdb-11e6-9456-444ab5211a2f (accessed 13 December 2017). On the new digital economy in Cambodia and Myanmar, see Peter Janssen, 'Small is beautiful, and profitable, in Cambodia', *Asia Times*, 17 March 2017, http://www.atimes.com/article/small-beautiful-profitable-cambodia/ (accessed 13 December 2017).

19 The 'digital nomad' lifestyle is building its institutional framework with specialized co-working spaces in hubs like Bali, Indonesia or Chiang Mai, Thailand. Sharing economy services like Roam (www.roam.com) are offering co-living arrangements where digital nomads can rent rooms with wifi connections and workspaces in any of the companies' different hubs worldwide. These are part of what FastCompany calls the digital nomad industrial complex, made up of 'networking, smartphone apps, the sharing economy, and on-demand services. Popular apps and services like Airbnb, WhatsApp, Yelp, Lyft, Duolingo, Earth Class Mail, and Google services like Maps and Translate'; see Mike Elgan, 'The digital nomad's guide to working from anywhere on earth', *FastCompany*, 22 February 2017, https://www.fastcompany.com/3068312/the-digital-nomads-guide-to-working-from-anywhere-on-e (accessed 16 November 2017). On the idea of post-captialist start-ups, see Boyd Cohen, *Post-Capitalist Entrepreneurship: Start-Ups for the 99 Per Cent*, London: CRC Press, 2017.

20 On the neo-artisan 'hipster economy' in the West, see Richard Ocejo, *Masters of Craft: Old Jobs in the New Urban*

Economy, Princeton, NJ: Princeton University Press, 2017. On the fusion of neo-artisan crafts and fashion, in London, Berlin and Milan, see Angela McRobbie, Dan Strutt, Carolina Bandinelli and Bettina Springer, *Fashion Micro-Enterprises in London, Berlin and Milan*, CREATe Working Paper 2016/13; on makers, see Massimo Menichinelli, Massimo Bianchini, Alessandra Carosi and Stefano Maffei, 'Makers as a new work condition between self-employment and community peer-production: insights from a survey on Makers in Italy', *Journal of Peer Production*, 10, 2017, http://peerproduction.net/issues/ issue-10-peer-production-and-work/peer-reviewed-papers/ makers-as-a-new-work-condition-between-self-employment- and-community-peer-production-insights-from-a-survey-on- makers-in-italy/ (accessed 17 November 2017). On Thai street fashion and its links to popular markets for low-quality fashions, see Adam Arvidsson and Bertram Niessen, 'Creative mass: consumption, creativity and innovation on Bangkok's fashion markets', *Consumption Markets & Culture*, 18(2), 2015, 111–32; on Indonesian street fashion, Brent Luvaas, 'Designer vandalism: Indonesian indie fashion and the cultural practice of cut'n'paste', *Visual Anthropology Review*, 26(1), 2010, 1–16; on Chinese shanzhai fashions, Sara Liao, 'Fashioning China: precarious creativity of women designers in Shanzhai culture', *Communication, Culture and Critique*, 10(3), 2017, 422–40.

21 On brands and the Shanzhai aesthetic, see Josephine Ho, 'Shanzhai: economic/cultural production through the cracks of globalization', *Keynote, Crossroads 2010 Cultural Studies Conference*, Hong Kong, 2010; Jeroen de Kloet, 'Europe as facade', *European Journal of Cultural Studies*, 17(1), 2014, 58–74; Nakassis, 'Counterfeiting what?' On aesthetics as emerging from dense face-to-face interaction in bazaars, see Maitrayee Deka, 'Bazaar aesthetics: on excess and economic rationality' (forthcoming). On the capitalist use of brands to structure markets, Adam Arvidsson, *Brands: Meaning and Value in Media Culture*, London: Routledge, 2006.

22 On Debian, see Coleman, *Coding Freedom*.

23 Douglas McWilliams, *The Flat White Economy*, London: Duckworth Overlook, 2015, p. 54. More generally McWilliams notes how 'the FWE [Flat White Economy] startup typically pays badly – just enough for the employee to subsist in a backpacker's lifestyle in London's expensive property market' (p. 31).

24 On Bangkok after the crisis in 1997, see John Walsh, 'The street vendors of Bangkok: alternatives to indoor retailers at a time of economic crisis', *American Journal of Economics*

and Business Administration, 2(2), 2010, 185–8; Claudio Sopranzetti, *Red Journeys: Inside the Thai Red-Shirt Movement*, Bangkok: Silkworm Books, 2012.
25 Max Weber, *The Protestant Ethic and the Spirit of Capitalism* (trans. S. Kalberg), Oxford: Oxford University Press, 2011 [1920], pp. 90, 177.
26 Michael Waltzer, *The Revolution of the Saints*, Cambridge, MA: Harvard University Press, 1965, pp. 308–16.
27 Frank H. Knight, *Risk, Uncertainty and Profit*, Chicago, IL: University of Chicago Press, 1971, p. 245. Cf. Joseph Schumpeter, *The Theory of Economic Development*, New Brunswick, NJ: Transaction Publishers, 2004 [1912]; Jens Beckert, 'Imagined futures: fictional expectations in the economy', *Theory and Society*, 42, 2013, 219–40. In his *Essai sur la nature du commerce en général (1755)*, Richard Cantillon, the first philosopher to use the term entrepreneur as an economic category, essentially equated entrepreneurship with precarity. In his analysis of the early eighteenth-century urban economy he distinguished between people who have a stable income, generally deriving from the state, like military officers and courtiers, and entrepreneurs whose existence is instead marked by fluctuating incomes and insecurity; see Giuseppe Berta, *L'enigma dell'imprenditore*, Bologna: il Mulino, 2018, pp. 15–19.
28 The quotes can be found in Chris Guillebeau, *The $100 Startup: Fire Your Boss, Do What You Love, and Work Better to Live More*, New York: Random House, 2012, p. xiv; Simon Sinek, 'Start with why', *Ted Talk*, 3 March 2014, https://www.youtube.com/watch?v=IPYeCltXpxw (accessed 3 January 2018). On Business Model Canvas, see Alexander Osterwalder and Yves Pigneur, *Business Model Canvas*, New York: Wiley, 2010.
29 McRobbie et al., *Fashion Micro-Enterprises*, pp. 16, 40; Adam Arvidsson, Giannino Malossi and Serpica Naro, 'Passionate work? Labour conditions in the Milan fashion industry', *Journal for Cultural Research*, 14(3), 2010, 295–309.
30 Adam Arvidsson, Alessandro Caliandro, Alberto Cossu, Maitrayee Deka, Alessandro Gandini, Vincenzo Luise, Brigida Orria and Guido Anselmi, 'Commons based peer production in the information economy', https://www.researchgate.net/profile/Alessandro_Caliandro/publication/310624903_Commons_Based_Peer_Production_in_the_Information_Economy/links/5834403108ae004f74c85030.pdf (accessed 11 May 2018); McRobbie et al., *Fashion Micro-Enterprises*, p. 40.

31 Ocejo, *Masters of Craft*, p. 134.

32 Surveys generally give different results. For example, a recent one of 19,000 21 to 36-year-olds in 25 countries suggests that millennials crave job security above almost all else: Sarah O'Connor, 'Job security is living the millennial dream', *Financial Times*, 26 May 2016, https://www.ft.com/content/8d22895a-20dc-11e6-aa98-db1e01fabc0c (accessed 3 January 2018).

33 See Carl Cederström and Peter Fleming, *Dead Man Working*, London: Zero Books, 2012; Carl Cederström and Andre Spicer, *The Wellness Syndrome*, Cambridge: Polity, 2015; Andre Spicer, *Business Bullshit*, London: Routledge, 2017. For reviews on the early literature on 'organizational cynicism', see James W. Dean, Pamela Brandes and Ravi Dharwadkar, 'Organizational cynicism', *Academy of Management Review*, 23(2), 1998, 341–52. Lynne M. Andersson and Thomas S. Bateman, 'Cynicism in the workplace: some causes and effects', *Journal of Organizational Behaviour*, 18(5), 1997, 449–69.

34 Regis Debray, *Le nouveau pouvoir*, Paris: Editions di Cerf, 2017; Alexis de Toqueville, *Democracy in America*, New York: Harper & Row, 1966 [1835]; Chris Lehmann, *The Money Cult: Capitalism, Christianity and the Unmaking of the American Dream*, London: Melville House, 2016.

35 Clayton Christensen, *The Innovator's Dilemma: When New Technologies Cause Great Firms to Fail*, Cambridge, MA: Harvard Business Review Press, 2013.

36 Lehmann, *The Money Cult*, p. 113.

37 Hartmut Rosa, *Social Acceleration: A New Theory of Modernity*, New York: Columbia University Press, 2013.

38 Alex Rosenblat, 'What motivates gig economy workers?', *Harvard Business Review*, 17 November 2016, https://hbr.org/2016/11/what-motivates-gig-economy-workers (accessed 22 February 2018).

39 Alfie Bown, *Enjoying it: Candy Crush and Capitalism*. Alresford, Hants: John Hunt Publishing, 2015.

40 Arvidsson et al., 'Commons based peer production', p. 29.

41 Alberto Cossu, 'Beyond social media determinism? How artists reshape the organization of social movements', *Social Media + Society*, 2018, doi 10.1177/2056305117750717.

42 See Luc Boltanski and Arnaud Equerre, 'The economic life of things: commodities, collectibles, assets', *New Left Review*, 98, March–April 2016, 31–54.

43 Vincenzo Luise, *Narrative, modelli e pratiche d'innovazione nell'economia start-up*, Milan: EGEA, 2019.

44 See Global Entrepreneurship Monitor 2016–17, p. 9; Feng Bing, Jingjing Chen and Huiqing Zheng, 'Who are they?

The small and micro entrepreneurs in Yiwu and Cixi', *Critical Arts*, 30(5), 2016, 689–708; Claudio Sopranzetti, 'Framed by freedom: emancipation and oppression in post-Fordist Thailand', *Cultural Anthropology*, 32(1), 2017, 68–92; Sanjay Srivastava, 'Fragmentary pleasures: masculinity, urban spaces, and commodity politics in Delhi', *Journal of the Royal Anthropological Institute*, 16(4), 2010, 835–52. On 'Instafame', Alice Marwick, 'Instafame: luxury selfies in the attention economy', *Public Culture*, 27(1), 2015, 137–60.

45 See, for example, Elizabeth Currid-Halkett, *The Sum of Small Things: A Theory of the Aspirational Class*, Princeton, NJ: Princeton University Press, 2017.

Chapter 4: Industrious Capitalism

1 On 'flexible specialization' and the return of industrious relations of production in 1970s restructuring, see Michael Piore and Charles Sabel, *The Second Industrial Divide: Possibilities for Prosperity*, New York: Basic Books, 1984; for the Italian debates, Giorgio Fuà and Carlo Zacchia (eds.), *Industrializzazione senza fratture*, Bologna: il Mulino, 1983.

2 On the growth of the urban service economy, see Saskia Sassen, *The Global City: New York, London, Tokyo*, Princeton, NJ: Princeton University Press, 2001; on links to the informal economy, see Alejandro Portes, Manuel Castells and Lauren Benton, *The Informal Economy: Studies in Advanced and Less Developed Countries*, Baltimore, MD: Johns Hopkins University Press, 1989.

3 Cheng Ting Fai, 'Foxconn unit to cut over 10,000 jobs as robotics take over', *Nikkei Asian Review*, 6 February 2018, https://asia.nikkei.com/Business/AC/Foxconn-unit-to-cut-over-10-000-jobs-as-robotics-take-over (accessed 10 January 2019).

4 Giangiacomo Bravo and Tine de Moor, 'The commons in Europe: from past to future', *International Journal of the Commons*, 2(2), 2008, 155–61.

5 Bonneuil and Fressoz, *The Shock of the Anthropocene*, p. 258.

6 See Antonio Negri, 'Il comune come modo di produzione', *UniNomade*, 10 June 2016, http://www.euronomade.info/?p=7331 (accessed 6 September 2017); Michael Hardt and Antonio Negri, *Empire*, Cambridge, MA: Harvard University Press, 2000; Massimo De Angelis, *The Beginning of History*: *Value Struggles and Global Capital*, London: Pluto Press, 2007; on the notion of 'vital subsumption', see

Andrea Fumagalli, *Per Un'economia politica del Comune: Sfruttamento e sussunzione nel capitlaismo bio-cognitivo*, Rome: DeriveApprodi, 2018.

7 Karl Marx, *Grundrisse*, London: Penguin, 1973, p. 705. The 'fragment on machinery' was first published separately as 'Frammento sulle macchine' (trans. Renato Solmi), in *Quaderni rossi*, 4, 1964. On tacit knowledge, see Michael Polanyi, *Personal Knowledge*, London: Routledge, 1958; on the contribution deriving from the formalization of informal or tacit knowledge during the industrial revolution, see Joel Mokyr, *The Gifts of Athena: Historical Origins of the Knowledge Economy*, Princeton, NJ: Princeton University Press, 2002. For a classic study of the importance of informal networks and skills even under Taylorist industrial management, see Donald Roy, 'Efficiency and the "fix": informal intergroup relations in a piecework machine shop', *American Journal of Sociology*, 60(3), 1954, 255–66.

8 Marx, *Grundrisse*, p. 705.

9 Marx, *Grundrisse*, p. 706, italics in original.

10 Marx, *Grundrisse*, pp. 705–6, italics in original.

11 Michael Hardt and Antonio Negri, *Commonwealth*, Cambridge, MA: Harvard University Press, 2009; Nick Dyer-Witheford, 'The circulation of the common', Immaterial Labour Conference, Cambridge, 29–30 April 2006, https://dlc.dlib.indiana.edu/dlc/.../4519/circulation%20of%20the%20common.pdf (accessed 6 September 2017).

12 See Armin Beverungen, Anna-Maria Murtola and George Schwartz, 'The communism of capital', *Ephemera*, 13(3), 2013, 484.

13 Fritz Machlup, *The Production and Distribution of Knowledge in the United States*, Princeton, NJ: Princeton University Press, 1973; Alfred D. Chandler, *The Visible Hand: The Managerial Revolution in American Business*, Cambridge, MA: Belknap Press, 1977. For an overview, see Armand Mattelart, *Networking the World, 1794–2000*, Minneapolis, MN: University of Minnesota Press, 2000.

14 See Arvidsson and Peitersen, *The Ethical Economy*, pp. 27–33.

15 Paul Adler and Charles Heckscher, 'Towards collaborative community', in Charles Heckscher and Paul Adler (eds.), *The Firm as Collaborative Community*, Oxford: Oxford University Press, 2006, p. 28.

16 Klaus Schwab, *The Fourth Industrial Revolution*, New York: Crown Publishing, 2016; John Hagel and John Seely Brown, *The Only Sustainable Edge*, Boston, MA: Harvard Business School Press, 2005.

17 Tom Peters and Charles Waterman, *In Search of Excellence: Lessons from America's Best-Run Companies*, Cambridge, MA: Harper & Row, 1982; similar arguments were preceded by Peter Drucker, *The Age of Discontinuity*, Cambridge, MA: Harper and Row, 1969; and Douglas McGregor, *The Human Side of Enterprise*, New York: McGraw-Hill, 1963. For an overview, see Luc Boltanski and Eve Chiapello, *Le nouvel esprit du capitalism*, Paris: Gallimard, 1999.

18 On the origins of the start-up/venture capital system in California's Silicon Valley (linked to the new and risky high-tech business of producing silicon microprocessor chips), see Martin Kenney, 'How venture capital became a component of the US national system of innovation', *Industrial and Corporate Change*, 20(6), 2011, 1677–723. The number of accelerator programmes for start-ups has increased tenfold in the US since 2008, from 16 to 170. In 2016 there were 579 accelerator programmes worldwide, investing \$200 million in 11,305 start-ups; see Catherine Clifford, 'Within 10 years, the number of accelerator programs in the US has increased tenfold', *EntrepreneurEurope*, n.d., https://www.entrepreneur.com/article/271000 (accessed 16 May 2018). The start-up economy is projected to grow fastest in Asia and Africa: Tom Jackson, 'Number of African tech startups funded rises 17% in 2016', *Disrupt-Africa.com*, http://disrupt-africa.com/2017/01/number-of-african-tech-startups-funded-rises-17-in-2016/ (accessed 16 May 2018).

19 On the tendency to postpone IPOs, see Rana Foroohar, 'Money, money, money: Silicon Valley speculation recalls dotcom mania', *Financial Times*, 17 July 2017, https://www.ft.com/content/968f2022-6878-11e7-9a66-93fb352ba1fe (accessed 16 May 2018); on the boom in private equity, Tom Braithwaite, 'Private investing is no solution to the ailing public market', *Financial Times*, 30 June 2017, https://www.ft.com/content/93ae0dbe-5d1a-11e7-b553-e2df1b0c3220 (accessed 16 May 2018). This dynamic is illustrated by the story of the Snapchat IPO in 2017; see Brooke Masters, 'Snap IPO is the foolish leading the blind', *Financial Times*, 3 March 2017, https://www.ft.com/content/60308fec-ff3d-11e6-96f8-3700c5664d30 (accessed 16 May 2018).

20 See Luise, *Narrative, modelli e pratiche d'innovazione nell'economia start-up*.

21 The figure comes from a private conversation with the head of a London-based high-tech incubator in October 2017.

22 Alex Rosenblat, 'The truth about how Uber's app manages drivers', *Harvard Business Review*, 6 April 2016, https://hbr.

org/2016/04/the-truth-about-how-ubers-app-manages-drivers (accessed 16 May 2018).

23 Neal Ungerleider, 'Hold the storefront: how delivery-only "ghost" restaurants are changing takeout', *FastCompany*, 20 January 2017, https://www.fastcompany.com/3064075/hold-the-storefront-how-delivery-only-ghost-restaurants-are-changing-take-out (accessed 16 May 2018).

24 'Why Southeast Asia is leading the world's most disruptive mobile business models', *Company Insights*, 23 May 2017, https://www.acommerce.asia/mobile-commerce-explosive-sales-channel-thailand/ (accessed 16 May 2018); Vinnie Lauria, 'LINE, WeChat, WhatsApp, Facebook: where most of Asia's business deals are being done', *Forbes*, 8 May 2017, https://www.forbes.com/sites/vinnielauria/2017/05/08/line-wechat-whatsapp-facebook-where-most-of-asias-business-deals-are-being-done/#2a03a8ec757f (accessed 16 May 2018); Michael Peel, 'Thailand motorbike taxi crackdown deals blow to Uber', *Financial Times*, 18 May 2016, https://www.ft.com/content/23f49294-1cc1-11e6-8fa5-44094f6d9c46 (accessed 16 May 2018). On vintage traders on Instagram, Carl Hamilton 'Seeing the world second hand: mad men and the vintage consumer', *Cultural Studies Review*, 18(2), 2012, 223–42.

25 Leon Kaye, 'Uber's subprime auto scheme is the last nail in the sharing economy's coffin', *TriplePundit*, 9 June 2016, https://www.triplepundit.com/2016/06/ubers-subprime-automobile-scheme-last-nail-sharing-economys-coffin/ (accessed 16 May 2018). On labour conditions in the platform economy, see Nick Srnicek, *Platform Capitalism*, Cambridge: Polity, 2017.

26 Chuck Jones, 'Apple's app store generated over $11 billion in revenue for the company last year', *Forbes*, 6 January 2018, https://www.forbes.com/sites/chuckjones/2018/01/06/apples-app-store-generated-over-11-billion-in-revenue-for-the-company-last-year/#163541726613 (accessed 16 May 2018).

27 The figure for Facebook like buttons comes from Mark Zuckerberg himself, who stated it in his 2018 congressional hearing; see https://clips.twitch.tv/SplendidCourageousPigGivePLZ (accessed 16 May 2018).

28 On Uber as an option for marginalized young men (mostly) in French *banlieues*, see Anne-Sylvaine Chassany, 'Uber: a route out of the French banlieues', *Financial Times*, 3 March 2016, https://www.ft.com/content/bf3d0444-e129-11e5-9217-6ae3733a2cd1 (accessed 16 May 2018); on Uber drivers in the US, see Sam Levin, 'Uber drivers often make below minimum wage, report finds', *The Guardian*, 6 March 2018, https://www.theguardian.com/technology/2018/mar/01/

uber-lyft-driver-wages-median-report (accessed 16 May 2018). While some platforms, like Uber or Grab in Asia, mainly use workers that come from the pre-existing service economy, others, like Airbnb or eBay, have attracted participants from the downwardly mobile middle classes; see Diana Farrell and Fiona Greig, 'Paychecks, paydays and the online platform economy', JP Morgan Chase Institute, 2016, https://www.jpmorganchase.com/corporate/institute/report-paychecks-paydays-and-the-online-platform-economy.htm (accessed 29 November 2017). Delivery services and platforms like TaskRabbit have a more mixed composition of the workforce, employing a significant amount of students and unemployed graduates. Nick Srnicek estimates that in the US in 2016, the workforce of TaskRabbit was composed of 70 per cent college graduates, Srnicek, *Platform Capitalism*, p. 81; on how underemployed college graduates in the US use TaskRabbit and other sharing platforms, see Nathan Heller, 'Is the gig economy working?', *The New Yorker*, 15 May 2017, https://www.newyorker.com/magazine/2017/05/15/is-the-gig-economy-working (accessed 29 November 2017); on how freelance creatives use platforms to get 'gigs', see Alessandro Gandini, Ivana Pais and Davide Beraldo, 'Reputation and trust on online labour markets: the reputation economy of Elance', *Work Organisation, Labour & Globalisation*, 10(1), 2016, 27–43.

29 Erin Griffith, 'More start-ups have an unfamiliar message for venture capitalists: Get lost', *The New York Times*, 11 January 2019, https://www.nytimes.com/2019/01/11/technology/start-ups-rejecting-venture-capital.html (accessed 15 January 2019).

30 For data on Facebook's economic performance, see 'Facebook reports fourth quarter and full year 2017 results', *Facebook Investor Relations*, 23 January 2018, https://investor.fb.com/investor-news/press-release-details/2018/facebook-reports-fourth-quarter-and-full-year-2017-results/default.aspx (accessed 18 May 2018); for Amazon, 'Annual reports, proxies and shareholder letters', *Amazon Investor Relations*, 18 April 2018, http://phx.corporate-ir.net/phoenix.zhtml?c=97664&p=irol-reportsannual (accessed 18 May 2018). On Amazon 'eating' the retail market, see 'Understand the retail apocalypse with one giant chart', *Stocktwitz*, 12 May 2017, https://blog.stocktwits.com/understand-the-retail-apocalypse-with-one-giant-chart-f9ce4434aa70 (accessed 18 May 2018).

31 On Uber, see Leslie Hook, 'Can Uber ever make money?', *Financial Times*, 23 June 2017, https://www.ft.com/content/09278d4e-579a-11e7-80b6-9bfa4c1f83d2 (accessed 18 May 2018); on Airbnb and its hedge fund, see Chris O'Brien, 'AirBnB

reportedly built an internal hedge fund that makes $5 million per month', *VentureBeat*, 7 February 2018, https://venturebeat. com/2018/02/07/airbnb-reportedly-built-an-internal-hedge-fund-that-makes-5-million-per-month/ (accessed 18 May 2018); on Uber Eats and other delivery platforms, Leslie Hook, 'Uber eats a bright spot on menu with $3 billion potential sales', *Financial Times*, 3 October 2015, https://www.ft.com/content/a40e56f2-b056-11e7-aab9-abaa44b1e130 (accessed 18 May 2018); on how labour conflict threatens the already meagre earnings of these companies, James Crisp, 'Deliveroo riders go on strike in Belgium and the Netherlands', *The Telegraph*, 20 January 2018, https://www.telegraph.co.uk/news/2018/01/20/deliveroo-riders-go-strike-belgium-netherlands/ (accessed 18 May 2018).

32 Michael K. Spencer, 'Silicon Valley is running out of juice', *Medium.com*, 11 October 2018, https://medium.com/futuresin/silicon-valley-is-running-out-of-juice-in-2018-978d0626231c (accessed 9 January 2019).

33 Salvador Rodriguez, 'The start-up economy is a "Ponzi scheme", says Chamath Palihapitiya', *CNBC*, 10 October 2018, https:// www.cnbc.com/2018/10/10/start-up-economy-is-a-ponzi-scheme-says-chamath-palihapitiya.html (accessed 7 January 2019). *Accelerator Report 2017*, http://gust.com/accelerator_reports/2016/global/ (accessed 18 May 2018). On the declining profitability of the start-up system, see Foroohar, 'Money, money, money'. For a comparative study of the economic performance of Italian start-ups, see Alessandro Gerosa and Adam Arvidsson, 'Start-up in Italia: limiti e potenzialità', *CheFare*, 7 February 2017, https://www.che-fare.com/start-up-italia-limiti-e-potenzialita/ (accessed 27 November 2017). On the 'magical thinking' that drives start-up investments, see Jennifer Brandel, Mara Zepeda, Astrid Scholz and Aniyia Williams, 'Zebras fix what unicorns break', *Medium.com*, 13 July 2017, https://medium.com/@sexandstartups/zebrasfix-c467e55f9d96 (accessed 18 May 2018).

34 On the Chinese social vision for digital platforms, see Anthony Li, 'Ecommerce and TaoBao villages', *Current Affairs: China Perspectives*, 3, 2017, 57–62; Louise Lucas, 'The Chinese Communist Party entangles big tech', *Financial Times*, 19 July 2018, https://www.ft.com/content/5d0af3c4-846c-11e8-a29d-73e3d454535d (accessed 21 August 2018); Teijun Wen, *Addressing Rural Development in Developing Countries: Lessons from the New Rural Reconstruction Programme in China*, Beijing: Institute for Chinese Studies, 2015.

35 Louise Lucas and Emily Feng, 'Inside China's surveillance state', *Financial Times*, 20 July 2018, https://www.ft.com/

content/2182eebe-8a17-11e8-bf9e-8771d5404543 (accessed 22 August 2018); Tsui Sit, Erebus Wong, Kin Chi Lau and Teijun Wen, 'One Belt, One Road: China's strategy for a new global financial order', *Monthly Review*, 68(9), 36–45; Xin Zhang, 'Chinese capitalism and the Maritime Silk Road: A world-systems perspective', *Geopolitics* 22(2), 2017, 310–31.

36 Arrighi, *Adam Smith in Beijing*; Hung, 'Imperial China and capitalist'.

37 David Bollier, 'Commoning as a transformative new paradigm', *The Next System Project*, 2016, http://thenextsystem.org/commoning-as-a-transformative-social-paradigm/ (accessed 21 September 2016); David Bollier and Silke Helfrich (eds.), *The Wealth of the Commons: A World Beyond Market and State*, Amherst, MA: Levellers Press, 2014; Massimo De Angelis, *Omnia Sunt Communia: On the Commons and the Transformation to Postcapitalism*, London: Zed Books, 2017. On the new role of social sharing, Benkler, *The Wealth of Networks*; Yochai Benkler, 'Sharing nicely: on shareable goods and the emergence of sharing as a modality of economic production', *Yale Law Jounal*, 114(2), 2004, 273–358; for a pioneering text on CBPP and its civilizational implications, see Michel Bauwens, 'The political economy of peer production', *CTheory*, 12(1), 2005.

38 Onthecommons.org,   http://www.onthecommons.org/about-commons#sthash.sh1envqu.dpbs (accessed 13 January 2018); Michel Bauwens, *P2P and Human Evolution: Peer to peer as the premise of a new mode of civilization*, http://wiki.p2pfoundation.net/P2P_and_Human_Evolution (accessed 13 January 2018). For an overview of the commons movement, see George Caffentzis and Silvia Federici, 'Commons against and beyond capitalism', *Upping the Anti*, 15, 2013, 83–91.

39 For a list of these various initiatives, see the 'repositories' at the P2PFoundation, curated by Michel Bauwens, http://wiki.p2pfoundation.net/Main_Page (accessed 20 May 2018).

40 On platform cooperatives, see Trebor Schultz, *Platform Cooperativism: Challenging the Corporate Sharing Economy*, New York: Rosa Luxemburg Stiftung, 2016. On alternative currencies, see Andrea Fumagalli and Emmanuele Braga, *La moneta del commune*, Rome: DeriveApprodi, 2015.

41 For more detailed results from the study, see Arvidsson et al., 'Commons based peer production in the information economy'.

42 On financial flows in the Shanzhai system, see Fu Lai Tony Yu and Diana S. Kwan, 'African entrepreneurs and interna-tional coordination in petty businesses: the case of low-end

mobile phones sourcing in Hong Kong', *Journal of African Business*, 16(1–2), 2015, 66–83; Meng Li, Suresh P. Sethi and Jun Zhang, 'Competing with bandit supply chains', *Annals of Operations Research*, 240(2), 2016, 617–40. On Shanzhai aesthetics as a parody of the dominant aesthetics of global brands, Barton Beebe, 'Shanzhai, sumptuary law and intellectual property law in contemporary China', *University of California, Davis Law Review*, 47, 2014, 849–74. On its role in Chinese popular culture and its link to nationalism, Lin Zhang and Anthony Fung, 'The myth of "Shanzhai" culture and the paradox of digital democracy in China', *Inter-Asia Cultural Studies*, 14(3), 2013, 401–16; Xi Cui, 'Discourse on Shanzhai cultural production in Chinese newspapers: authenticity and legitimacy', *Chinese Journal of Communication*, 5(4), 2012, 399–416; Winnie Won Yin Wong, 'The Panda Man and the anti-counterfeiting hero: art, activism and appropriation in contemporary China', *Journal of Visual Culture*, 11(1), 2012, 20–37; and overall, Ho, 'Shanzhai: economic/cultural production through the cracks of globalization', pp. 17–21. On the links between Shanzhai and the new wave of Chinese quality brands, see 'Shenzhen is a hothouse of innovation', *The Economist*, 8 April 2017, https://www.economist.com/news/special-report/21720076-copycats-are-out-innovators-are-shenzhen-hothouse-innovation (accessed 4 September 2017).

43 See Lindtner et al., 'Designed in Shenzhen'.
44 Valérie Fernandez, Gilles Puel and Clément Renaud, "The Open Innovation paradigm: from outsourcing to open-sourcing in Shenzhen, China', *International Review for Spatial Planning and Sustainable Development*, 40(4), 2016, 27–41.
45 Martin Arnold, 'Tech start-ups raise $1.3 billion this year from initial coin offerings', *Financial Times*, 18 July 2017, https://www.ft.com/content/1a164d6c-6b12-11e7-bfeb-33fe0c5b7eaa (accessed 4 September 2017); Izabella Kaminska, 'Silicon Valley's cryptocurrency craze is a bubble in the making', *Financial Times*, 18 July 2017, https://www.ft.com/content/b12dd3ea-6ba9-11e7-bfeb-33fe0c5b7eaa (accessed 4 September 2017); Jack du Rose, 'Why Ethereum startups don't need San Francisco or Silicon Valley', *VentureBeat*, 1 July 2017, https://venturebeat.com/2017/07/01/ethereum-startups-dont-need-silicon-valley/ (accessed 4 September 2017); Luke Thompson, 'No slowdown for ICO investments amid cryptocurrency selloff', *AsiaTimes*, 9 August 2018, http://www.atimes.com/article/no-slowdown-for-ico-investments-amid-crypto-currency-selloff/ (accessed 30 August 2018). On community-based

investments for bitcoin-based infrastructure projects, see 'The Bitcoin model of crowdfunding', StartupBoy, 9 March 2014, https://startupboy.com/2014/03/09/the-bitcoin-model-for-crowdfunding/ (accessed 30 August 2018); James Burke, 'Next stage in ICOs: the community token economy', Medium.com, 3 September 2017, https://medium.com/outlier-ventures-io/the-next-stage-in-icos-the-community-token-economy-cte-995cfb043136 (accessed 21 August 2018). On current attempts to use blockchain technology to build commons-based market systems, see, for example, Alexander Lange, 'Mapping the decentralized world of tomorrow', Medium, 1 June 2017, https://medium.com/birds-view/mapping-the-decentralized-world-of-tomorrow-5bf36b973203 (accessed 4 September 2017); Arthur Brock and Eric Harris-Braun, 'Mutual credit cryptocurrencies: beyond blockchain bottlenecks', White Paper CEPTR, http://ceptr.org/whitepapers/mutual-credit (accessed 1 September 2017). On the token economy as an 'escape' from the venture capital system and on its ability to sustain a new labour markets, see Richard Burton, 'The people and their protocols', Medium.com, 20 June 2017, https://medium.com/balance-io/the-people-and-their-protocols-dce03bb5b704 (accessed 25 August 2018).

Chapter 5: A New Industrious Revolution?

1 Rosa, *Social Acceleration*, p. xxxix.
2 Eric Hobsbawm, *The Age of Revolution, 1986–1848*, London: Weidenfeld & Nicolson, 1962.
3 The exercise will be quite unorthodox from a historian's perspective for at least two reasons. I will treat the 'industrious revolution' as an economic as well as a social and cultural phenomenon, and I will push its roots much further back than usual. On the early modern industrious revolution in Europe and Asia, see Jan de Vries, 'The industrial revolution and the industrious revolution', *The Journal of Economic History*, 54(2), 1994, 249–70; Kaoru Sugihara, 'The East Asian path of economic development: a long-term perspective', in Giovanni Arrighi, Takeshi Hamashita and Mark Selden (eds.), *The Resurgence of Asia: 500, 150 and 50 Year Perspectives*, New York: Routledge, 2004. On the East Asian early modern 'industrious revolution', see Christopher A. Bayly, *The Birth of the Modern World, 1780–1914: Global Connections and Comparisons*, Oxford: Blackwell, 2004; Carol H. Shiue and Wolfgang Keller, 'Markets in China and Europe on the eve of

the Industrial Revolution', *American Economic Review*, 97(4), 2004, 1189–216; Stephen Broadberry, 'Accounting for the Great Divergence', LSE Economic History Working Papers, no. 184, 2013.

4 On Weber's suggestion that the English puritans were at the vanguard of the industrial revolution, see Weber, *The Protestant Ethic*, p. 175; for a later validation of the argument, Joel Mokyr, *Culture of Growth: The Origins of the Modern Economy*, Princeton, NJ: Princeton University Press, 2017.

5 Weber discusses Sombart's suggestions and critique in note 12 to the Second Chapter of *The Protestant Ethic*; see Weber, *The Protestant Ethic*, pp. 292–3; for a more systematic account of medieval antecedents of Weber's protestant ethic and in particular the industrious attitude that stands at the centre of it, see Pierre Musso, *La religion industrielle*, Paris: Fayard, 2017. There has since been many attempts to 'de-centre' Weber's argument, showing that a similar inner-worldly industrious orientation could be found among, for example, Hindu businesses elites in the seventeenth century; see, for example, Jack Goody, *The East in the West*, Cambridge: Cambridge University Press, 1996. On the influence of magic and natural philosophy on the protestant inner-worldly orientation, see Christopher Hill, *The World Turned Upside Down: Radical Ideas during the English Revolution*, London: Temple Smith, 1972; Chris Lehmann, *The Money Cult: Capitalism, Christianity and the Unmaking of the American Dream*, London: Melville House, 2016.

6 Robert I. Moore, *The First European Revolution, c.970–1215*. Cambridge: Blackwell, 2000, p. 10.

7 Robert S. Lopez, *The Commercial Revolution of the Middle Ages 950–1350*, Cambridge: Cambridge University Press, 1976; Marc Bloch, *Feudal Society*, Chicago, IL: University of Chicago Press, 1965.

8 Lopez, *The Commercial Revolution*, p. 139; see also Janet Abu-Lughod, *Before European Hegemony: The World System AD 1250–1350*, Oxford: Oxford University Press, 1989; David Abulafia, *The Great Sea: A Human History of the Mediterranean*, London: Penguin, 2011, pp. 287–317.

9 On the category of 'masterless men' and their social importance in the Middle Ages and the Early Modern period, see Norman Cohn, *The Pursuit of the Millennium: Revolutionary Messianism in Medieval and Reformation Europe and its Bearing on Modern Totalitarian Movements*, New York: Harper, 1961. On urbanization, Paul Hohenberg and Lynn H. Lees, *The Making of Urban Europe, 1000–1950*, Cambridge,

MA: Harvard University Press, 1985. Roberto Lopez suggests that the success of the Italian maritime cities can be partially explained by their freedom, while their rivals in France or Spain depended on the power of lords or kings. Feudal lords in general had to strike a balance between the desire to tax towns and in particular the periodic fairs that remained important throughout the Middle Ages, and the danger of killing off this new golden goose, or moving it elsewhere, Lopez, *The Commercial Revolution*, pp. 130–1.

10   Cohn, *The Pursuit of the Millennium*, p. 41.

11   On the development of commercial law, the role of the corporations and the social and economic thought of the Italian *umanisti civili*, see Oscar Nuccio, *La storia del pensiero economico italiano*, Rome: Luiss University Press, 2008; on Franciscan economic ideas and early attempts to creat a 'civic economy', see Bruni and Zamagni, *Economia Civile*, 2004; on Albertanus of Brescia, see James M. Powell, *Albertanus of Brescia: The Pursuit of Happiness in the Early Thirteenth Century*, Philadelphia, PA: University of Pennsylvania Press, 1992; on the role of guilds in supporting a new more 'modern' civil society centred on notions of freedom and equality, see Anthony Black, *Guilds and Civil Society in European Political Thought from the Twelfth Century to the Present*, London: Routledge, 1984; Bert De Munck, 'From brotherhood community to civil society? Apprentices between guild, household and the freedom of contract in early modern Antwerp', *Social History*, 35(1), 2010, 1–20. See also, Max Weber, *The City*, New York: Free Press, 1958.

12   Jean Birrell, 'Common rights in the medieval forest: disputes and conflicts in the thirteenth century', *Past & Present*, 117(1), 1987, p. 22.

13   Tine de Moor, 'The silent revolution: a new perspective on the emergence of commons, guilds and other forms of corporate collective action in Western Europe', *Internationaal Instituut Voor Sociale Geschiedenis* 53(Supplement), 2008, 179–212, p. 185; Peter Linebaugh, *The Magna Carta Manifesto*, Berkeley, CA: University of California Press, 2008.

14   de Moor, 'The silent revolution', p. 197; also Bo Gustafsson, 'The rise and economic behavour of medieval craft guilds: an economic theoretical interpretation', *Scandinavian Economic History Review*, 35(1), 1987, 1–40.

15   John R. Maddicott, 'Magna Carta and the local community 1215–1259', *Past & Present*, 102, 1984, p. 25.

16   On proto-industry, see Peter Kreidte, Hans Medick and Jurgen Schlumbohm, *Industrialization before Industrialization*, Cambridge: Cambridge University Press, 1981.

17 On the role of the guilds in the medieval economy, see Lopez, *The Commercial Revolution*, pp. 156–65; on their importance in paving the way for market society, see Avner Grief, *Institutions and the Path to the Modern Economy: Lessons from Medieval Trade*, Cambridge: Cambridge University Press, 2006. For a summary of the debates on the role of petty producers in the transition to capitalism, see Robert Brenner, 'Dobb on the transition from feudalism to capitalism', *Cambridge Journal of Economics*, 2(2), 1978, 121–40; Immanuel Wallerstein, 'From feudalism to capitalism: transition or transitions?', *Social Forces*, 55(2), 1976, 273–83.

18 Weber cites the eighteenth-century economist and philosopher Sir William Petty on the role of the puritans in driving Dutch economic growth in the seventeenth century and the run-up to the English industrial revolution in the late eighteenth century; Weber, *The Protestant Ethic*, pp. 175, 392 (note 106). Contemporary support for these arguments can be found in de Vries, 'The industrial revolution and the industrious revolution' (although an additional motivating factor was new access to consumer goods), and Mokyr, 'Entrepreneurship and the Industrial Revolution in Britain'. On the empowerment of popular culture and its political role in the eighteenth century, see Peter Burke, *Popular Culture in Early Modern Europe*, New York: Harper & Row, 1978, p. 269. On Magna Carta and the English Revolutions, see Linebaugh, *The Magna Carta Manifesto*.

19 According to many recent environmental historians, the Black Death was not simply a contingent event but its impact was made possible by declining agricultural productivity in Europe and, in particular, by the onset of the Little Ice Age in the fourteenth century bringing a wetter and colder climate across Europe that lasted well into the nineteenth century. As Patel and Moore write: 'The Little Ice Age laid bare feudalism's vulnerabilities. Its food system, for example, worked well only while the climate remained stable. This was chiefly because the system ran through a particular class arrangement, in which lords enjoyed formal control over the land and peasants cultivated it. Lords oversaw a rising peasant population, which was able to generate a rising surplus, with a tendency towards diminishing returns. Soil fertility was slowly exhausted over the centuries, a decline partially concealed by a rising population of peasants wringing the last out of fixed areas of land. When the climate turned it created a cascade of failures, propagated through a class system that enforced soil exhaustion and starvation, killing millions.' Patel and Moore, *History of the*

World in Seven Cheap Things, pp. 9–10. On the spread of market relations in the countryside and its role in undermining feudal hierarchies, see Perry Anderson, *Passages from Antiquity to Feudalism*, London: New Left Books, 1974, p. 202; Martin Empson, *Kill All the Gentlemen: Class Struggle and Change in the English Countryside*, London: Bookmarks Publications, 2018.

20 Jason W. Moore, 'The crisis of feudalism: an environmental history', *Organization & Environment*, 15(3), 2002, 301–22; on the guilds as a source of 'post-apocalyptic' innovation, see Sevket Pamuk, 'The Black Death and the origins of the "Great Divergence" across Europe, 1300–1600', *European Review of Economic History*, 11(3), 2007, 289–317; Guy Bois, *Crise du féodalisme*, Paris: Presses de la Fondation National des Sciences Politiques, 1975.

21 For an overview, see Charles Sabel and Jonathan Zeitlin, 'Historical alternatives to mass production: politics, markets and technology in nineteenth-century industrialization', *Past & Present*, 108, 1985, 133–76.